Synod Extraordinary

The inside story of the Rome Synod
November–December 1985

PETER HEBBLETHWAITE

Doubleday & Company, Inc.
Garden City, New York
1986

Library of Congress Cataloging in Publication Data

Hebblethwaite, Peter.
  Synod Extraordinary.
  1. Catholic Church, Synod Extraordinary (1985:
Rome, Italy) 2. Catholic Church—History—1965–
I. Title.
BX837.5.H42 1986   262'.136   85–27160
ISBN 0–385–23466–X

Contents

Prefatory Note

sýn'od, noun (from Greek *sunodos*, *SYN-hodos*, common way). An ecclesiastical meeting, usu. involving bishops, of the Church in a country, a region or a jurisdiction. E.g. the S. of Arles c.493 (condemned 'semi-pelagianism') or the S. of Whitby in 664 (Celtic monks accept 'Western' Church practices).

For the Greek Orthodox, the S. is an advisory body made up of twelve bishops, four of whom are residential while the rest live permanently in Constantinople (Istanbul); it resembles, therefore, the *Roman Curia*. For the Presbyterians, the S. is a court above presbyteries and subject to the General Assembly. For the Lutherans (esp. in the US) synodical government has led to splits between more or less liberal factions (e.g. the Missouri S.). Invented in 1970, the Anglican S. is the most democratic; made up of elected representatives from the house of bishops, clergy and laity; diocesan S. feed the General S.; the 1985 elections produced the General S. that will sit until 1989. For Roman Catholics, the setting up of the S. of bishops by Pope Paul VI in 1965 was in response to requests made at Vatican Council II (1962–5) that *collegiality* should be continued after the Council. It has three forms.

An *ordinary* S. has met (at first) every two years and (since 1971) every three years; each *episcopal conference* elected delegates according to its numbers: the US has four, England and Wales two, Scotland only one; some religious superiors are added, and the Pope may nominate up to fifteen per cent more members. A *special* S. is devoted to the affairs of a particular region or church; there have been three so far: the Netherlands (1980) and two for the Ukrainian Catholic church (1980 and 1985). An *extraordinary* S. differs from an ordinary S. in that its membership is restricted to Presidents of Episcopal Conferences or their equivalents; all the heads of Roman *dicasteries* attend; but as for an ordinary S., the Pope sets the agenda, appoints the officials, determines its duration and (since 1978) writes its document; in 1969, an extraordinary S. discussed the *reception* of *Humanae Vitae*.

This book tells the story of the Extraordinary S. of 1985, beginning on a snowy day in January.

1

A Surprise Announcement

On 25 January 1985, feast of the conversion of St Paul, Pope John Paul II went to the basilica of St Paul without the Walls to conclude the annual octave of prayer for Christian unity. That was conventional enough. But the Pope chose this occasion to make the surprise announcement that he was summoning an Extraordinary Synod for the end of the year. Since this address was for a long time our only source for understanding the purpose of the Synod, it is here given in full:

At the end of this eucharistic celebration of the feast of the conversion of St Paul, which finds us gathered here by the glorious tomb of the apostle, at the conclusion of the octave of prayer for Christian unity, an event comes to the consciousness of each one of us. This year marks the twentieth anniversary of the conclusion of the second Vatican Council, the first announcement of which, we well recall, was given by my predecessor John XXIII of venerable memory here in this basilica, on this same date, 25 January 1959.

The second Vatican Council remains the fundamental event in the life of the contemporary Church. It was fundamental for deepening of the wealth entrusted to her by Christ. In her and through her he extends and imparts to mankind the *mysterium salutis*, the mystery of salvation, the work of redemption. It was fundamental for fruitful contact with the contemporary world, for the purpose of evangelization and dialogue at all levels with all people of upright conscience. I had the special grace of participating in the Council and actively collaborating in its development. For me the second Vatican Council has always been – in a particular fashion during these years of my pontificate – the constant reference point of every pastoral action, with conscious commitment to translate its directives into concrete, faithful action, at the level of every church and of the whole Church.

We must ceaselessly refresh ourselves at that source, and all the more when meaningful dates, such as those of this year, grow near, and stir memories and emotions from that truly historic event.

Today therefore, on the feast day of the conversion of St Paul, with deep joy and emotion, I call an extraordinary general assembly of the Synod of bishops, which will be celebrated from 25 November to 8 December of the present year, and in which the patriarchs and a number of archbishops of the eastern churches and presidents of all episcopal conferences of the five continents will take part.

The aim of this initiative is not only that of commemorating the second Vatican Council twenty years after its conclusion, but is also and above all:

to revive in some way the extraordinary atmosphere of ecclesial communion which characterized that ecumenical assembly, through mutual participation in sufferings and joys, struggles and hopes, which pertain to the Body of Christ in the various parts of the earth;

to exchange and deepen experiences and information concerning application of the Council at the level of the universal Church and the particular churches;

to favour further deepening and constant application of the second Vatican Council in the Church's life, also in the light of the new needs.

I attribute particular importance to this extraordinary assembly of the Synod. That is the reason why I have chosen to make public announcement of it in this basilica today, here where announcement of the ecumenical Council of our century first resounded. The intention moving me follows in the line of that of my venerated predecessors John XXIII and Paul VI: to contribute to that 'renewal of thoughts, activities, behaviour, and moral force and joy and hope, which was the very same purpose of the Council'.

From now on I entrust realization of the Extraordinary Synod of bishops to the prayers of the Church and the powerful inter- cession of SS Peter and Paul, and with you above all I implore the immaculate Virgin, Mother of the Church, that she may assist us in this hour and obtain for us that fidelity to Christ of which she is the incomparable model through her readiness to be 'the handmaid of the Lord', and through her constant openness to the Word of God.

In this total fidelity and perseverance the Church of today wills to pursue her way towards the third millennium of history, in the midst of mankind and with it, sharing in men's own hopes and expectations, following the path traced out by the second Vatican Council, and always listening to 'what the Spirit says to the churches'.

So Pope John Paul was consciously emulating what his predecessor had done twenty-six years before. John Paul's decision was sudden, unexpected and – it was hinted – inspired. Its meaning seemed clear enough on a first rapid reading. His commitment to the Council was firm and unhesitating ('the constant reference point of every pastoral action', etc.). The threefold purpose of the Synod – reviving the atmosphere of the Council, exchanging information about its implementation, and applying it to the new needs that had arisen – seemed admirable and uncontroversial. And yet before the hosannas could ring out, there were already doubts and hesitations about what the Extraordinary Synod would really mean in practice.

The first and major doubt flowed from the hasty nature of the announcement. Everything suggested that this was a last-minute idea impulsively decided upon without any consultation. This was proved by a curious little *lapsus* made by John Paul. He said that Pope John had announced the Council 'here in this basilica' (*qui in questa basilica*). But every informed person knew that Pope John did not announce the Council in the basilica of St Paul without the Walls. The announcement was made privately at a cardinals-only meeting in the chapter-house of the adjoining abbey. This was a trivial slip, no doubt, but it proved that John Paul had not submitted the text of his address to anyone serious in the Roman Curia. The Cardinal Secretary of State, Agostino Casaroli, would have at once corrected the blunder. Therefore he had not seen it.

Archbishop Jozef Tomko, Slovak Secretary of the Synod Council, probably was consulted; but his memory was even faultier than the Pope's for he began his first press conference on the Synod with two erroneous statements that did not inspire confidence:

Many people still recall that memorable evening of 25 January 1959, in the majestic basilica of St Paul without the Walls, when Pope John XXIII, with his air of courageous simplicity, made the historic announcement of an ecumenical Council. The unexpected news had the effect of a lightning bolt out of a clear sky. (*L'Osservatore Romano*, 5 February 1985)

Pope John began his announcement at ten past one. That was hardly evening by any stretch of the imagination.

There is no need to labour the point further. There was little informed consultation and the project had simply not been thought through. The Pope launched his own lightning bolt out of a clear blue sky, and then set off the next day for a twelve-day visit to Latin America, leaving Rome-based reporters floundering. The new Vatican press officer, an Opus Dei lay Spaniard, Joaquin Navarro-Valls, showed his hand by banning Domenico Del Rio of *La Repubblica* from the papal plane. No charges were specified but he had been mildly critical of the usefulness of papal journeys. Those who were on the plane asked Casaroli where the idea of the Synod had come from. 'It was all his own idea', he replied with an imperceptible flicker of his right eyebrow. It was what every bureaucrat does when picking up the pieces for an unpredictable chief. 'Don't blame me', was his implicit comment. Casaroli then resumed the inscrutable air he uses when dealing with the Chinese.

Editors and journalists all round the world had to make up their minds swiftly about what the calling of the Synod meant. They all agreed that it was a surprise. Yes, Pope John Paul had pulled it off again. His election was a surprise – the first non-Italian for 457 years; the reactivation of the college of cardinals as a consultative body was another surprise; the summoning of the Dutch bishops to Rome in January 1980 for a special Synod was a surprise; and so was the decision to designate 1983 a Holy Year. For someone who is so often justly considered to be a traditionalist, John Paul shows a striking readiness to do what is unorthodox or at least unprecedented. Everyone chorused that the calling of the Extraordinary Synod was another papal surprise.

Unanimous in declaring the Synod a surprise, the Catholic press immediately diverged as to its interpretation. In the absence of hard information this was only to be expected. The views of the British Catholic press are not unrepresentative. Let us start with them.

The Universe, which boasts of being 'the largest religious newspaper in the country' (127,452 was its last declared figure), cried in a bold headline: BISHOPS WELCOME VATICAN II SYNOD; although their Rome correspondent could find only three (or just possibly four) bishops to quote to justify the optimistic headline. The paper's editorial, under the banner 'The Spirit of Vatican II', confidently declared:

Poor Pope John Paul has done it again!

4

By inviting the bishops of the Church to meet him in Rome in November to discuss Vatican II, some 'experts' have decided his intention is to neutralize, if not undo, the work of the Council. Of course these experts are 'liberals' who have for a long time decided that because the Pope does not agree with their views he must be a reactionary autocrat who wants to lead the Church backwards.

Pope John Paul has made it very plain that he has called the Synod to relive the spirit of Vatican II. The Pope is not putting question marks against this commitment.

He knows that the Church must go on renewing itself and growing in knowledge. Of necessity, this involves an evaluation of what has been happening in the past twenty years.

An autocratic, reactionary Pope would have done this alone. (*The Universe*, 1 February 1985)

This was neither imperceptive nor crude. But it did beg certain questions. By putting 'experts' and 'liberals' in quotes, it suggested that the 'experts' were frauds and the 'liberals' merely partisan bigots. It recalled the traditional Catholic usage of the 1930s when one had to refer to the 'so-called' Reformation – meaning it was not really a 'reformation' at all. *The Universe* did not allow for the possibility that there might be genuine experts or even authentic liberals who legitimately thought that the pontificate was in danger of becoming a dazzling solo performance or a one-man band.

The Catholic Herald failed to comment editorially straight off, no doubt wisely, but in a news item it perpetrated more mistakes than Tomko had made. Asterisks indicate them:

> Standing at the same altar* at which Pope John had announced the second Vatican Council, Pope John Paul in an equally unexpected move has called a special* Synod of world bishops to meet in Rome in November to discuss the decisions of the Council 'in the light of new needs'. . . .
>
> Synods are normally held at three-year intervals and the next, on youth*, is due in 1986. However, special* Synods have been convoked in the past, the most recent being that of the Dutch bishops in Rome in 1980. (*The Catholic Herald*, 1 February 1985)

The reader can already spot some of the errors here. Nor is it merely pedantic to add that the theme of the 1986 Synod (soon to be transferred to 1987) was never 'youth' but rather 'The Vocation and Mission of the Laity in the Church and in the World' – a very different kettle of fish. Nor had Pope John Paul II convened a 'special synod', which concerns a region or a nation, but rather an 'extraordinary synod' involving the whole Church but on a particular question.

It was left to *The Tablet*, founded in 1840 and therefore the oldest Catholic paper in Britain, to ask the right questions. In an editorial headed 'The Challenge to the Bishops', it declared:

> This is an opportunity which the bishops must seize. The Pope wants to know their opinion of his analysis of the Council. They have a duty to be frank. For many bishops feel that full effect is not being given to the exercise of collegiality. Whereas Vatican II laid emphasis on the team, Pope John Paul lays it on the captain. (*The Tablet*, 2 February 1985, p. 103)

This was uncannily prophetic. The English and Welsh bishops would seize their opportunity exactly in the manner recommended by John Wilkins, editor of *The Tablet*. It alone contrived to set the calling of the Extraordinary Synod in the context of the pontificate as a whole. As seen by the London paper, the grounds for disquiet were threefold, here numbered for convenience:

1. The Synod of bishops has never fulfilled its collegial promise. The Synod of the family of 1980 was a particular disappointment. The bishops went to Rome and voiced the concerns of their people in an exhilarating spirit of freedom and honesty. Yet the Pope's concluding address seemed to take little account of their deliberations, and a year later the papal document *Familiaris Consortio* contained no allusion to a number of recommendations the bishops had made. . . .

2. The truth is that the papacy of Pope John Paul II has not yet acquired a real ecumenical dimension. Whereas Paul VI was conscious that he himself was part of the problem, Pope John Paul II has so far given no sign that this awareness is included in his experience of office. . . . Today other Christians are closely watching how Rome is exercising its office, and they do not like what they see.

3. The Pope remains committed to the Council, as he again affirmed this week. Through it, he said, 'the Holy Spirit speaks to us'. But the whole trend of his papacy testifies to his reservations. They arise because he feels that in opening its arms to the world, the Church let the world in too much, thus blunting

6

the cutting edge of its proclamation. (*The Tablet*, 2 February 1985, p. 103)

I did not write this editorial. I rather wish I had. It got the scenario right from the outset. Through the maze of British understatements *The Tablet* was simply saying that the Extraordinary Synod would have to be understood not in isolation but in the context of the pontificate as a whole. Looked at from that point of view, the omens were not good. Indeed, some were positively sinister.

For Cardinal Joseph Ratzinger, Prefect of the Congregation for the Doctrine of the Faith (the former Holy Office), had become the chief ideologue or guru of the pontificate. His views carried weight. And in an interview in *Jesus*, a magazine belonging to the right-wing organization *Communione e Liberazione*, Ratzinger declared war on the way the Council had been interpreted.

He claimed to know from private reports that the Church was plainly 'collapsing' in various unspecified regions. He described Karl Rahner's notion of 'anonymous Christians' (which pointed out that since all grace is the grace of Christ, any good work done by a non-believer is inspired by Christ and must be referred to him) as 'a dangerous catch-phrase'. The slippery notion of 'the Spirit of the Council' had become, he declared, 'an anti-Spirit, an incubus'. Warming to his theme, Ratzinger concluded that certain theologians (so far anonymous) had 'feminized God', attacked his fatherhood under the specious influence of Sigmund Freud, and been excessively optimistic about the chances of goodness existing in this sublunary world. As for the Council, though good 'in itself', it had led to all manner of unbridled excesses. What was needed was a 'restoration' of lost pre-conciliar values.

It seemed a short logical step from talking of the need for 'restoration' to actually repudiating Vatican II. For as Paul Valadier sj was to say (in *Etudes*, October 1985), there is not much point in declaring that Vatican II is fine but, alas, its fruits are bitter and inedible. The Gospel text is simply: 'By your fruits you shall know them'. Ratzinger will recur in these pages and, indeed, have a whole chapter devoted to him. One reason for alarm at this early stage was that with his interview he appeared to have set the agenda of the Extraordinary Synod.

The fact that Ratzinger was the chief watchdog of orthodoxy in this pontificate led to the pessimistic early responses to the Synod. The silencing of Fr Leonardo Boff, the Brazilian Franciscan and liberation theologian, on 11 February 1985 seemed to confirm this gloomy judgement. Besides, it was noticed that when Pope John Paul visited Peru, he made no attempt to enter into dialogue with the best-known Peruvian, Father Gustavo Gutierrez, an Indian priest whose 1971 book *A Theology of Liberation* earned him the title of 'father of liberation theology'. He had not invented it; it was in the air; what mattered was that he had named it. Ratzinger had tried to persuade the Peruvian bishops to condemn Gutierrez, but, divided among themselves, they had so far failed to comply. So Ratzinger's interview and actions combined to arouse fears that 'the clock was about to be put back'.

This phrase was used in several reports from Rome. It was attributed to 'a Belgian theologian in the Vatican'. Since there are not too many Belgian theologians in the Vatican, he ought to have been easily identifiable. But what the anonymous Belgian said in regret was confirmed in delight by curial Cardinal Silvio Oddi, as reported by Desmond O'Grady:

> Preparation for the Synod must be hurried and Cardinal Silvio Oddi, hard-line Prefect of the Congregation for the Clergy, gave a hint of what delegates can expect by immediately stating that there are post-conciliar errors to be corrected. (*The Catholic Herald*, 1 February 1985)

Taken seriously, that would make the task of the Synod exactly the opposite of Vatican II which, according to Pope John, was not called to correct errors. As he charmingly remarked in his inaugural speech on 11 October 1962, 'errors often vanish as quickly as they arise, like mist before the morning sun'. He meant that an obsession with 'errors' is a bad sign. It is the mark of the inquisitor. It has little to do with the Gospel.

Time magazine found a somewhat better source than Oddi. Its informant explained:

> In the face of criticism that the Pope is turning the clock back to pre-conciliar days, one of his closest advisers declares that this is a misinterpretation of the papal views. John Paul, says this observer, looks to the future, viewing his mandate in terms of three core-concepts. They are *integrality, identity* and *clarity*: the integrality of the Christian message; the identity of the priests and nuns who present it; and, above all, clarity that will let everyone know exactly what the Church stands for. (*Time*, 4 February 1985)

One could wish this 'closest adviser' had been named. After all, he

8

said nothing discreditable. He could come out of the closet without blushing. Quite clearly, anyway, this anonymous 'deep purple' was Jan Schotte, shortly to become Secretary of the Synod Council. The language and the concepts are his.

They are question-begging. What, for example, is the 'integrality' of the Christian message being contrasted with? Does he mean that some theologians only give half the message or try to adulterate it to suit modern tastes? If so, one ought to distinguish between that sort of reductionism and the legitimate attempt to present the heart or gist of Christian faith unencumbered by the dusty bric-à-brac of centuries. Moreover, deep purple's suggestion that the Christian message is entrusted exclusively to 'priests and nuns' is slanderous of the laity whose role in the Church and the world was to be the topic of the next ordinary Synod. And, finally, while the demand for clarity is understandable, total clarity can never be expected in religious matters which begin in submission to the mystery which God enacts in the midst of his people. Said the head of the papal household, the witty Frenchman, Mgr Jacques Martin: 'The Pope wants everything in black and white, but it is impossible to be both truthful and diplomatic at the same time'.

Bishops with pastoral responsibilities revealed none of the pessimism of the Roman officials. Their comments were almost wholly positive. Cardinal Basil Hume said: 'After twenty years, the Extraordinary Synod provides an opportunity for the local churches to rededicate themselves to the continuing implementation of the Council'. Besides being Archbishop of Westminster and the President of the Episcopal Conference of England and Wales, Hume was also President of the Council of European Bishops' Conferences. So his words carried extra weight and prefigured the policy he would consistently carry out.

The Americans agreed with him. Cardinal Joseph Bernadin of Chicago saw the Synod as 'an opportunity for renewal' (in which, however, he would take part only if invited by the Pope, which did not happen). The President of the United States Catholic Conference (USCC), Bishop James W. Malone of Youngstown, Ohio, said the Synod's purpose would be 'to apply the wisdom and insights of the Council to the present day'. Cardinal Vicente Enrique y Tarancón, retired Archbishop of Madrid, remarked that 'if the Pope had wanted to reimpose an authoritarian style on the Catholic Church, he would have done it in an authoritarian way, not by calling a consultation'. True: but ten days did not seem to leave much time for a serious consultation. US Jesuit Avery Dulles, son

9

of President Eisenhower's Secretary of State and Professor at the Catholic University, Washington, discounted the alarmist view. He told *The New York Times*:

> If anybody thinks this is some kind of disavowal of the Council, I would regard this interpretation as certainly wrong. There is a certain amount of disaffection with the Council from the extreme right and the extreme left, but I don't think the Pope identifies with either of them.

The New York Times headline for 2 February neatly encapsulated the problem: 'Vatican Synod: Timing Dramatic, Intent Unclear'.

These were all very early reactions to an event which would acquire both momentum and meaning in the course of the next ten months. The truth of the matter was that neither cardinals nor learned Jesuits were in a position to comment in an informed fashion about a Synod whose significance was far from evident. The unexpected papal announcement caught them on the hop.

Or to change the metaphor, it set up a huge blank screen on which everyone could cast his or her hopes or fears, convictions or apprehensions, about Vatican II and the state of the Roman Catholic Church in 1985. But precisely because the project was so vague and ill-defined, these early comments represented an attempt to hijack the Synod and make sure it went in the 'right' direction. As Clifford Longley remarked in *The Times*, most early episcopal comments were 'two thirds speculation and one third jockeying for position' (4 February 1985).

With a little hindsight, one can see that something much deeper was at stake. What the Synod had to consider was the 'reception' of Vatican II. 'Reception' is a technical theological term which, in practice, is a synonym of efficacy. A Council may be said to have been 'received' when it has been accepted and implemented. The Council of Florence, for example, in the fifteenth century produced an agreement between Latins (Catholics) and Greeks (Orthodox) which would have put an end to the schism started in 1054. But the agreement could not be made to stick. It was rejected. It failed. It was not 'received'.

Even Councils that were undoubtedly 'received' (at least in the West) needed time to be accepted, understood and put into practice. The Council of Trent ended in 1563, but its liturgical reforms were not fully complete until 1614, over fifty years later. However, the concept of 'reception' made Catholic theologians nervous because Vatican I (1870) declared that conciliar statements were valid 'of themselves, and not because of the subsequent consent of the Church'. In other words, you did not have to wait to see how a doctrine was 'received' before knowing it was true. One thinks of *Humanae Vitae*. But Vatican I's shaft was aimed at the French or Gallican church which (in the past) had pronounced papal edicts invalid until they had been confirmed by the local church. 'Reception' did not mean that.

All it meant was that time was needed for conciliar teaching to trickle down and sink into every corner of the Church. And twenty years was not a long time. So the question before the Synod would be: how is the process of 'reception' going?

Professor Giuseppe Alberigo, Director of the Institute of Religious Studies in Bologna University, published a collection of essays with the very topical title *La Réception de Vatican II* (Paris, 1985). Unfortunately, it omitted to discuss the concept of 'reception' itself. For that we still have to turn to the classic article by Yves-Marie Congar OP, *'La "réception" comme réalité ecclésiastique'* in *Revue de Sciences Philosophiques et Théologiques* (56, 1972, pp. 369–403).

But the Alberigo volume does contain a splendid essay by Gustavo Gutierrez who is here not wearing his 'theology of liberation' hat. He is just 'being a theologian in the post-conciliar Church'. His judgement would represent mainstream theological orthodoxy. He could easily take up a chair in Louvain where he once studied with Godfried Danneels, now Cardinal Archbishop of Malines-Brussels.

Though the title of Gutierrez's essay is 'The relationship between the Church and the poor as seen from Latin America', it is in fact a solid piece of work on what Pope John XXIII intended his Council to do. This was, after all, a rather important question. For unless one knew why he had called the Council, one had no criteria for judging whether it had succeeded or failed in realizing his aims.

Gutierrez made three simple points about Pope John's intentions.

1. Pope John wanted the Church to learn from the world. This was a condition of teaching it. The Holy Spirit was at work in the Church, but he was also at work 'out there', in the men and women and movements of our time. John called this sympathetic listening 'discerning the signs of the times'. Discerning means seeing in difficult circumstances. It does not mean splashing holy water indiscriminately on everything that is going on or giving in to trendy fads. This 'signs of the times' approach was embodied in *Gaudium et Spes*, the conciliar constitution on the Church and the modern world, and *Dignitatis Humanae*, its decree on religious liberty.

11

2. The second object of the Council as conceived by Pope John was ecumenical. True, the separated brothers were present only as observers, not as participants. But 'observer' suggests a passivity that was simply not the case; and even hidebound conservatives found it more difficult, though not actually impossible, to caricature those who were sitting on the other side of St Peter's. The result was that the Council stressed what united Christians rather than what divided them, conceded that the ecumenical movement was of the Holy Spirit (the Christian way of saying it was a Good Thing), and tried to remind Catholics that they were Christians by declaring that there was 'an order or "hierarchy" of truths according to their connection with the fundamentals of Christian doctrine' (*Unitatis Redintegratio*, 11).

3. Gutierrez maintained that the Council realized Pope John's hopes on these two questions. The third was less consistently carried through. It was the emphasis on the Church as the Church of the poor. Pope John had used this term just a month before the Council in his 11 September 1962 broadcast. It will be illuminating, he said, to present the Church 'in the under-developed countries as the Church of all, and especially of the poor'. *Gaudium et Spes* picks up this emphasis in its opening sentence which expresses a willingness to share in the joys and hopes of all mankind, but 'especially those who are in any way poor or afflicted'. This was the starting-point for liberation theology with its 'option for the poor'. It was 'post-conciliar', but it carried forward what the Council had promised and applied it to Latin America where, humanly speaking, as Pope John Paul has agreed, the future of the Church is being played out.

These three 'tests' of the efficacy (or 'reception') of Vatican II, written before the Extraordinary Synod was even dreamed of, provided three useful criteria by which one could judge whether the Synod would 'put the clock back' or not. If any of them were attacked, one would have a right to be worried; if all were repudiated, Vatican II would indeed have been buried. At his first press conference, Archbishop Tomko challenged the sceptics to examine the record of Karol Wojtyla both during and after the Council. They would discover, he averred, that no one was more pro-Vatican II than the former Cardinal Archbishop of Krakow, now Pope John Paul II. The next chapter will examine that proposition, documents in hand.

2

Karol Wojtyla and the Council

When Pope John announced the Council on 25 January 1959, Karol Wojtyla was a mere thirty-eight. He had been made auxiliary Bishop of Krakow in July 1958, in the last months of the pontificate of Pius XII. His appointment seems to have surprised himself as much as his friends. Both as bishop and professor of a Catholic university, he was invited to submit ideas for the agenda of the coming Council. He produced a seven-page text (*Acta et Documenta Concilio Vaticano II Apparando, Series I, Antepreparatoria, vol. II, part II,* Rome, 1960, pp. 741–8). His suggestions reflect both his Polish background – apart from two years in Rome in 1946–8 he had lived nowhere else – and the phenomenological studies on which he had been engaged as philosophy teacher in the Catholic University of Lublin. Professionally he was more of a philosopher than a theologian.

Writing in December 1959, Karol Wojtyla thought that the most important task facing the Council would be to make a clear statement on the transcendence of the human person against the growing materialism of the times. The human person has absolute dignity because made in the image and likeness of God. Ethics and the good life (*beata vita*) are impossible without inter-personal relations, which for their fullness require access to the life of the Trinity. Wojtyla thought it was important to bring out clearly the difference between this Christian 'personalism' and other forms of 'personalism'. He noted that some had 'faith' of a sort in humanism, but pronounced it fragile and easily tipped over into its contrary, despair.

Wojtyla believed that the doctrine of the Mystical Body of Christ was the key to thinking about the unity of the Church. There can only be one Body, one Church of Christ. The members of the Body may be fit or unfit, but they remain related to the Body. They can be sick with heresy, a sin against faith; or afflicted by schism, a sin against charity. This was the orthodox interpretation of *Mystici*

13

Corporis (1943). It was unable to fit the 'separated brethren' into its scheme of things. It did not have a 'sin against hope'.

Turning to more practical matters, Bishop Wojtyla pointed out that canon law (that is the code promulgated in 1917) had deplorably little to say about the laity. The Council ought to lay down the theological basis for the participation of lay people in the life of the Church and the world. Finally Wojtyla had a section on priestly discipline in which the duty of celibacy was reasserted and linked with the privilege of saying Mass. There were proposals for breviary reform and – a more personal note – a request that priests should take an interest in sport and the theatre in order discreetly to 'sacralize' these activities. Other themes such as liturgical reform and ecumenism were briefly touched on.

It must be confessed that these proposals for the Council written in Krakow in December 1959 were not exactly earth-shaking. They were more interesting than what came from Southwark, England, where the Archbishop assured his flock in a pastoral letter that the 'Last Gospel' (chapter 1 of St John) would remain for ever and that the Council – he had it on good authority – would declare Our Lady Mediatrix of All Graces. Wojtyla did rather better than that.

But his proposals do not reveal any trace of that enthusiasm for the Council that was found, for example, in popular works such as Hans Küng's *The Council and Reunion*, which had so much influence in the West. One has to say that Karol Wojtyla did not have very high expectations of the Council. He hoped for a better presentation of the Catholic faith in a world perceived as hostile; he wanted a Council of reaffirmation.

In this he was behaving as one would expect a Polish bishop to behave. This was not because Polish bishops were ignorant of the outside world or, as the cliché has it, outstandingly 'conservative'. As the Polish bishops took their place once more in the universal Church – and it was touch-and-go whether they would be allowed to go to Rome at all – they were disconcerted: the very first session of the Council in autumn 1962 seemed to confirm the fears of Cardinal Stefan Wyszynski, the Primate, that this event was going to make life immensely more difficult for the Polish bishops.

It was after all a basic rule of their episcopal conference that they should meet in secret, reach their decisions in private, and then announce them to the world as unanimous. This has remained the attitude of Pope John Paul, who told the West German bishops in November 1980 that it was an illusion to imagine that a squabbling hierarchy was more credible than an harmonious one.

But the first session of the Council blew a great, gaping hole in the Polish theory. It showed bishops arguing fiercely about almost everything. It drew up precise battle-lines: the liberal stars like Giacomo Lercaro (of Bologna) and Léon-Joseph Suenens (of Malines-Brussels) were applauded in the *aula*, especially among the younger bishops at the bottom of the nave where Wojtyla sat, while curialists like Alfredo Ottaviani were treated with disdain and on occasions derision. This shocked the Polish bishops. And it was all being reported in gruesome detail in the Western press. The Polish government could exploit these divisions in Rome to prove that the united front of the Polish bishops at home was a thinly painted-over façade.

By the second session, autumn 1963, there was a new pope, Paul VI, who had spent six months in Poland in 1923 (that was better than nothing), and a fresh difficulty. Pope John's encyclical, *Pacem in Terris*, his last will and testament, had appeared to embarrass them. For it was more tolerant of communism than they were prepared to be, making a distinction between its theory and its *praxis*:

> True, the philosophic formulation does not change once it has been set down in precise terms, but the programme clearly cannot help being influenced to some extent by the changing conditions in which it has to be worked out. What is more, who can deny the possible existence of good and commendable elements which do indeed conform to the dictates of right reason and are an expression of legitimate human aspirations? (*Pacem in Terris*, no. 159).

This troubled the Polish bishops for two reasons. First, they did not really believe it, for it did not correspond to their experience: communism was not evolving in the optimistic direction forecast by Pope John. Second, it presented the Polish government with a splendid propaganda card: it could contrast good Pope John, peace-loving and progressive, with the fuddy-duddy stick-in-the-mud Polish hierarchy. It was the city council, not the Catholics, who erected a statue to Pope John in Wroclaw. Moreover, *Pacem in Terris* was also a hint to the Council on how it should approach the Church's relationship to 'the world'. So whichever way one looked at it, the Council posed a threat to the Polish bishops.

It is difficult to evaluate with any precision Karol Wojtyla's personal contribution to the Council. He spoke nine times in the *aula* and made thirteen written interventions. His remarks in commissions mostly escape us. He may not always have chosen his topics: some were assigned to him by the secretariat of the Polish bishops.

However, his remarks on ecclesiology show that he had inched forward since penning his suggestions in December 1959. Four years on he no longer proposed the Mystical Body as the determining 'model' of the Church and accepted that 'People of God' was a better starting-point. He also agreed with the majority that the chapter on the People of God should come before that on the hierarchical nature of the Church. This was significant because it meant that one started from the radical equality in grace of all the baptized before making distinctions based on office in the Church; and so office – including that of the Petrine ministry – was seen not as power or privilege but as a service to the community as a whole. In short, office was ministry (23 October 1963). Wojtyla also denounced lay passivity and insisted – again reflecting Polish conditions – that they should be concerned as much with the individual lay apostolate as with Catholic Action, the lay movement which 'Latins' invariably thought of when they heard 'lay apostolate' mentioned. But he had nothing to say about collegiality.

On the other hand, he was eloquent on religious liberty – one of the most fiery topics the Council handled. Here again there was a contrast between West and East. Europeans and North Americans were bothered about religious liberty because they knew that without it there could be no ecumenism. The nineteenth-century thesis still being defended by Ottaviani (motto: *Semper idem*, 'Always the same'), that 'error has no rights', would have to be dropped; and the principled way to do it, said Cardinal Augustin Bea, aided not a little by American Jesuit Fr John Courtney Murray, was to show that only persons could have (or not have) rights and that 'error' as such was an abstraction. Pope John had already said this in *Pacem in Terris*: one must distinguish between the error (always wrong, always to be condemned) and the person who is in error (always to be respected). So religious freedom for the West was something that the Church was belatedly conceding to its new-found ecumenical partners. But in Poland religious liberty was rather something that the Church claimed from a reluctant government.

Wojtyla made a characteristic speech on religious liberty on 22 September 1965. He insisted that the text should emphasize 'the responsibility to seek the truth' as much as the freedom to pursue it. He wanted it to be made clear that there were some 'limits' to religious liberty, some concessions that could not be made for fear of falling into 'indifferentism' ('It doesn't matter what you believe'). But where were these limits?

One of them was 'public order': religious people should not be allowed, for example, to commit mass suicide as the crazed sect were to do in Guyana. However, the Poles did not like this criterion of 'public order' because it was precisely what their government used as a cloak for its arbitrary acts of repression. You cannot hold a mass pilgrimage because that would be 'against public order'.

On 20 September 1965 Wyszynski thundered away against the draft proposed by Mgr Pietro Pavan (known to have worked on *Pacem in Terris*, and therefore already suspect of being soft on communism) which spoke limply of 'public order in conformity to juridical norms'. Other formulations were essayed: 'public order based on true equity'; 'a well-ordered and just social order'; and 'public order, founded in the objective moral order'. According to Bishop Emile De Smedt of Bruges, Karol Wojtyla at this point proposed 'in conformity with the objective moral order' (Jan Grootaers, *De Vatican II à Jean-Paul II*, 1981, p. 159), a reference to the natural law which very nearly scraped home. The final version says simply: 'Nor is the exercise of this right to be impeded, provided that the just requirements of public order are observed' (*Dignitatis Humanae*, 3). The final draft of the whole document was revised to allow for a long list of Polish objections prepared by Karol Wojtyla. If he influenced any document of the Council directly, it was the decree on religious liberty.

Yet it is commonly believed his biggest contribution was to *Gaudium et Spes*. This half-truth leads to the question raised by Archbishop (as he then was) Tomko: how can Pope John Paul possibly reject a document of which he was an author? But the true story is rather more complicated.

Karol Wojtyla became Archbishop rather than auxiliary of Krakow early in 1964 – this gave him more authority – and towards the end of May that year he submitted to the Presidency of the Council a completely new version of the 'Church and world' text. The Polish bishops, in short, were so dissatisfied with the existing draft (known as Schema XIII) that they proposed to scrap it and replace it with a new one. The 'Polish proposal', as it was known, was unacceptable because the other draft had been approved and was already on the agenda for the third session. But it is worth looking at the Polish proposal to see what a Wojtyla-inspired *Gaudium et Spes* might have looked like:

1. the basis of the Church's presence in the world;
2. the aims of the Church in the world;
3. the mission of the Church in the world;
4. the chief means of realizing this mission in the contemporary world, that is, the witness of faith, individual Christian life, Catholic associations, relations with non-Christians and civil society. (Grootaers, p. 161)

One notes the deductive method: it begins from above, and the 'world' is merely the target of the Church's care; and the 'signs of the times' are simply not there. Sometimes Pope John Paul reaches nostalgically back to this 1964 'Polish proposal'.

But in 1964, though the Polish bishops' alternative scheme was rejected, their views had somehow to be accommodated, so in September Wojtyla was invited to join the 'signs of the times' working group. Its task was to describe, as objectively as could be, the changes or 'mutations' that characterized the modern world. What features made it different? What, indeed, made it 'modern'? Wojtyla's presence in this working group meant that these mainly West European theologians could no longer claim to speak for the whole world; the topic would have to be broken down, for manifestly there were vastly different 'worlds'. Wojtyla was given the task of describing 'the communist world'. This is what he wrote:

1. in some ways, e.g. in technology and industrialization, the 'communist world' has something in common with the 'first world';
2. communism can also be found 'outside' its own 'world' (e.g. in Italy);
3. the principal feature of the 'communist world' is the constraints it places on personal and social liberty;
4. the 'communist world' is atheistic;
5. this document, Schema XIII, is of the greatest importance for those who live in the 'communist world'; the Schema seeks to begin a dialogue with the contemporary world, in which the communists are perhaps the most difficult partners; but they are fascinated by the idea of dialogue and above all by what the Church will say about its relationship with the world; so for us, this document is much more important than many others. (Grootaers, pp. 161–2).

Wojtyla repeated the idea that one had to allow for the diversity of 'worlds' in the *aula* on 24 October 1964, when he made what has

18

frequently been regarded as his most 'progressive' contribution to the conciliar debates. He objected to the 'tone of voice' of the draft. He wanted a less schoolmasterly tone, and some sign that the Church was engaged with others in the search for solutions to human problems. I paraphrase rather than translate, because Wojtyla's language is difficult. He calls this method 'heuristic', for example, which he defines as 'allowing the pupil to find the truth as it were on his own' (*permittendo discipulo veritatem quasi ex suis invenire*) (*Acta Synodalia Concilii Vaticani II*, 1975, vol. III, part V, p. 299). His epigram that sometimes those who embarked on dialogue ended up by delivering monologues sounded sensible enough and earned him a place on the 'Mixed Commission' called upon to produce yet another 'final' draft of Schema XIII.

Fr Roberto Tucci, now head of Vatican Radio and impresario of papal trips after Archbishop Paul Marcinkus' police-enforced retirement, remarked that Wojtyla, even though he did not have a vote, was an assiduous member of the mixed commission and plied it with notes. But time was running out. Towards the end of September 1965, as the final session began, the ten sub-commissions were reorganized, and Karol Wojtyla found himself helping to write chapter 4 which concluded part I. Its title 'On the role of the Church in the modern world' (*De munere Ecclesiae in mundo hujus temporis*) summed up the whole document and was therefore of crucial importance. (It is still chapter 4 and has the same title in *Gaudium et Spes*; see Abbott, ed., *The Documents of Vatican II*, 1966, pp. 238–48.)

One says Wojtyla 'helped to write' this chapter, and so he did in the sense that he was a member of the team that wrote it. But this does not mean he liked it. Indeed on some vital questions, he was in a minority. We know this because when this very chapter came before the Council, he attacked it with some relish. He said the draft lacked 'a sense of Christian realism'. He thought 'the human person' should have been the corner-stone of the document, but it was not. He was afraid that creation was emphasized at the expense of the doctrine of redemption. He felt that the idea in this chapter 4, that the Church could and should learn from the world, could blur the distinction between them and obscure the specific task of the Church.

In all this Wojtyla was echoing what might be called the 'German' tendency at the Council. While the French were 'optimistic' and inclined to see God's grace at work in the secular movements of the age (a favourite theme of the French Dominicans

Yves-Marie Congar and Marie-Dominique Chenu), the Germans stressed human sinfulness and the folly of the Cross. French optimism was symbolized by Teilhard de Chardin, whose influence on *Gaudium et Spes* is clearly perceptible. Already, however, Teilhard was criticized not only by Ottaviani at the Holy Office (who had secured a wholly ineffectual *monitum* against him – reading Teilhard can damage your health – in the summer of 1962) but, more ominously for the future, by Hans Urs von Balthasar, the Swiss ex-Jesuit, who charged that Teilhard allowed his doctrine of creation to overwhelm the doctrine of redemption. That was exactly what Karol Wojtyla said in the *aula* of St Peter's in September 1965.

So already in 1965 there was an argument between optimists and pessimists. It has to be said that the optimists won in 1965, but were less sure of carrying the day in 1985. Here I will interpolate a memory from 1965 which throws light on the optimism–pessimism debate.

One day in October Fr Jean Daniélou sj emerged from St Peter's and gave an impromptu press conference on its steps. In his extraordinary high-pitched voice, Daniélou declared:

> The fathers are discussing Schema XIII on the relationship of the Church to the world. Some say it should be more optimistic while others say it should be more pessimistic. The optimists are mostly Frenchmen, yes, my compatriots, who have read too much Teilhard de Chardin. They are like good boy scouts. They smile and whistle all the time. The pessimists are mostly Germans: they have read too much Martin Luther and they are profoundly aware of the terrible ravages of sin. They are sunk in gloom. And I myself, what do I myself think? Should Schema XIII be more optimistic or more pessimistic?

Here Daniélou paused for dramatic effect, as the little knot of reporters wondered on which side he would come down. Having done a few Gallic shrugs to indicate the importance and difficulty of this question, he finally vouchsafed: 'But I myself do not agree with any of them. I say Schema XIII should be both *more optimistic* and *more pessimistic*, and therefore' (another pause) '*more dramatic*'. I suspect Daniélou got it about right.

As the Council drew to an end, groups of bishops went to say farewell to Pope Paul VI. When the Polish bishops met him on 13 December 1965, he could hardly believe his ears as the Polish primate, Cardinal Wyszynski, a man whose prison experience lent him immense prestige at home, voiced his disquiet about the Council:

> We are aware that it will be very difficult, but not impossible, to put the decisions of the Council into effect in our situation. There-fore we ask the Holy Father for one favour: complete trust in the episcopate and the church of our country. Our request may appear very presumptuous, but it is difficult to judge our situation from afar. Everything that occurs in the life of our church must be assessed from the standpoint of our experience. . . . If one thing is painful to us, it is the lack of understanding among our brothers in Christ. (Quoted in Hans-Jakob Stehle, *Eastern Politics of the Vatican 1917–1979*, 1981, pp. 341–2)

Paul coolly replied that he had no doubt the Council would be implemented 'energetically and willingly' in Poland as well as else-where. As he looked round the thirty-eight Polish bishops, it must have seemed to him that the young Archbishop of Krakow might fulfil the task the Primate found so difficult. That may explain why Wojtyla was made a cardinal in 1967, against precedent.

But of course Cardinal Wojtyla could not implement the Council single-handedly in Poland. He would have to work within the constraints and at the rhythm of the episcopal conference. It was a deliberately slow business. Wyszynski believed that Poles would be upset by the mariology of the Council which, though sober and clear, was dictated – he maintained – by an undignified concern for what Protestants would think. Nor did the Council encourage pilgrimages, one of the most characteristic forms of Polish piety. The Council talked about the pilgrim Church; the Poles went on pilgrimages.

There was another obstacle to over-hasty 'implementation' of the Council in Poland: there was for a long time no edition of the Polish translation of the sixteen Council documents. This was partly caused by government restrictions on the paper supply; but another factor was the slowness of the 'official' translation. The result was that most Poles knew very little about the Council. It was a remote event happening in another world. It was not the transforming experience it had been elsewhere.

So Cardinal Wojtyla's book, *U Podstaw Odnowy*, originally published in Krakow in 1972 (and translated as *Sources of Renewal* in 1980), really introduced Polish Catholics to the ideas of the Council for the first time. It presents an idiosyncratic version of what happened:

The Council had a unique and unrepeatable meaning for all who took part in it, and most particularly for the bishops who were Fathers of the Council. These men took an active part for four years in the proceedings of the Council, drafting its documents, and at the same time deriving great spiritual enrichment from it. The experience of a world-wide community was to each of them a tremendous benefit of historic importance. The history of the Council, which will one day be written, was present in 1962–5 as an extraordinary event in the minds of all the bishops concerned: it absorbed all their thoughts and stimulated their sense of responsibility, as an exceptional and deeply felt experience. (*Sources of Renewal*, p. 9)

So that was the 'experience' evoked by Pope John Paul on 25 January 1985. That was the harmonious and uplifting spiritual experience they would be trying to recapture at the Synod.

It is a moving picture. But it is incomplete. The Council appears as wholly content-less, as though what was said does not matter compared with the mere fact of meeting. Again, the Council is presented as though it were the private spiritual experience of bishops, as though it had not aroused expectations among almost everyone in the Church. And finally, one would never suspect from these bland and high-minded memories that harsh words were ever exchanged at the Council, or that at times there was uproar in St Peter's. Even Halina Bortnowska, a Polish theologian who edited a more digestible and popular version of *Sources of Renewal*, says:

Sources of Renewal was a first and provisional sketch. The author hides behind numerous quotations from the Council. . . . The Council texts and they alone occupy the stage and there is *no appeal to post-conciliar or even conciliar discussions*. One has a feeling of great abstractness and remoteness from the world of people seeking some guidance for their lives. (*L'Arrichimento della Fede*, Vatican Press, 1981, p. 17, my italics)

It is possible that the abstract feel noted by Bortnowska is explained by the fact that Wojtyla was professionally a philosopher. In his major philosophical work, *The Acting Person*, he makes this revealing remark:

While writing this book [in the first, Polish version], the author attended the second Vatican Council and his participation in the proceedings stimulated and inspired his thinking about the person. It suffices to say that one of the chief documents of the

Council, the pastoral constitution on the Church in the modern world, not only brings to the forefront the human person and his calling, but also asserts the belief in his transcendent nature. The constitution asserts: 'The role and competence of the Church being what it is, she must in no way be confused with the political community, nor bound to any political system. For she is at once the sign and safeguard of the transcendence of the human person'. (*The Acting Person*, 1979, pp. 302–3, fn. 9. the quotation from *Gaudium et Spes* comes from no. 76)

We have already seen that when invited to submit suggestions for the Council agenda, Karol Wojtyla proposed 'the transcendence of the human person'. It is not surprising, then, that he should pick this out as one of its most important points. He may, indeed, have insisted on the insertion of this passage. We all tend to remember our own contributions best.

Yet it is difficult to see why a council was needed to assert 'the transcendence of the human person'. It was after all the bedrock of Catholic social teaching, and it had been proclaimed in countless encyclicals. The problem lay not in asserting but in 'cashing' it: what, concretely, did it mean in wartime Poland or contemporary South Africa? It would be hard to claim its reassertion as a major breakthrough by Vatican II. Yet that was what Karol Wojtyla did.

This brings out another feature of his account of the Council. His version stresses continuity rather than a break with the past, reassurance rather than challenge, perduring identity rather than novelty. So the 'reception' of the Council in Poland differed from its reception elsewhere. In the Netherlands, for example, the Council was experienced as a liberation. In France people were more inclined to believe that the rest of the Church had just caught up with them. The quality of the 'reception' of the Council depended on previous expectations. But in Poland expectations were low. And they were outbalanced by apprehensions.

Thus, while theologians in the West were, as they used to say, 'exploiting the new insights of Vatican II', Cardinal Karol Wojtyla was telling Poles that the Council had been an intense spiritual experience. One only has to compare *Sources of Renewal* with, say, Bishop Christopher Butler's *Theology of Vatican II* (1967), to become keenly aware of the difference. Moreover, Wojtyla was already engaged in polemics with these Western theologians. He believed that they were not just rocking the boat but holing it underwater.

In 1971 Wojtyla gave an address to the Polish Theological Association on the theme 'Theology and theologians in the post-conciliar Church'. The entire lecture was devoted to the relationship between theologians and bishops. But that was over six years ago. Since then the relationship had soured. The proper task of theologians, he declared, was to 'guard, defend and teach the sacred deposit of revelation' in close association with but also strict subordination to the bishops. The role of theologians is merely 'consultative' (Roman jargon for saying they cannot settle anything). So the charge was that theologians were 'usurping the teaching function in the Church'. There would have been no reason to say all this unless he believed that something had gone badly wrong somewhere.

He was not – he explained – talking about Poland but about 'certain circles, especially in the West' which dismissed Polish theology as 'conservative' while themselves falling into 'false irenicism, humanism and even secularism'. Not much imagination was needed to conclude that the target of this attack was the multi-language review, *Concilium*. The Polish bishops rejected a proposal for a Polish translation of *Concilium* (which originated in Holland) saying that it was unnecessary: Polish theologians were polyglot. But in the minds of the Polish bishops this move prevented theologians like Hans Küng, Edward Schillebeeckx and Karl Rahner from emptying the churches of Poland as they were deemed to have emptied those of the West. When in 1972 Swiss theologian Hans Urs von Balthasar began to produce a counterblast to *Concilium* (he called it *Communio*), it was soon translated into Polish. So hostility to theologians as a class is part of Karol Wojtyla's make-up. He conceded them only a minor role in the Council itself and blames them for the subsequent 'post-conciliar crisis'. This is very much what Cardinal Joseph Ratzinger also believes. Though he was a member of the board of *Concilium* at the start, he soon fled to safer pastures.

The upshot of this chapter is that Karol Wojtyla's experience of the Council was very intense but also very personal. Most of his fellow bishops have given a different account. The diaries that are now beginning to be published confirm that they are right. The historian will regard Karol Wojtyla as a good witness to the Polish response to the Council. But one cannot rewrite history simply because he has become Pope.

It follows that what Pope John Paul was trying to conjure up with the Extraordinary Synod was not exactly what others would have meant, desired or remembered. The same language is used to cover different purposes. Declarations of fidelity to the Council did not always mean what they appeared to mean. Still, there was always the possibility that Karol Wojtyla might have been changed by his election as Pope. Indeed, he told the diplomatic *corps* on 18 October 1978 that 'the particular nature of our country of origin is from now of little importance; as a Christian, and still more as Pope, we are and will be witnesses of universal love'.

A noble ambition, but difficult to realize.

3

An Agenda takes Shape

As we saw in chapter 1, Pope John Paul's unexpected announcement on 15 January 1985 left everyone flummoxed. An examination
of his writings before he became Pope has still not decisively answered the question: what did he intend by calling an Extraordinary
Synod to commemorate Vatican II? On 19 February 1985 Archbishop Jozef Tomko gave a press conference which, it was hoped,
would clear up confusions, quell speculations and explain all.
Tomko was Secretary of the Synod Secretariat, the body which in
principle ensures continuity from one Synod to the next. He had
only one predecessor, the Polish Archbishop (now Cardinal) Wlad-
yslaw Rubin. Though no one knew it at the time, this was to be
Tomko's swan-song. A few weeks later he was made a Cardinal
and appointed Prefect of Propaganda (now rebaptized as the
Congregation for the Evangelization of Peoples) following the
sudden death after less than a year in the saddle of Archbishop
Dermot Ryan, the former Archbishop of Dublin.

Tomko offered the following explanation for the summoning of
the Extraordinary Synod. 'To pass up in silence', he declared, 'an
event of such richness as the second Vatican Council, might be seen
as contributing to the "burial" of the Council.' But it could perfectly
well have been commemorated by a speech or an academic session.
Then it would not have been 'passed up in silence'. An Extraordinary Synod was an expensive way to reach the same goal.

In any case, there is something rather arbitrary about which
anniversaries are kept. In the same year, 1985, most of Europe
'celebrated' forty years after the end of World War II; but in Japan
the same commemoration took on darker and more tragic hues. It
is good that wars come to an end, but not with the first use of
atomic bombs. But why choose ten, twenty or forty years? There is
nothing magical about two decades. One theory had it that Pope
John Paul, having noticed how the Congregation for Divine
Worship celebrated the twentieth anniversary of *Sacrosanctum Conci-*

lium, the constitution on the liturgy, in October 1984, decided to have one big celebration. Otherwise all the Roman congregations would try to organize their own: an unlikely story. Asked to explain the reasoning behind twenty years, Cardinal Basil Hume gravely explained to Kevin O'Kelly of Irish Radio (RTE), with a twinkle in his eye, 'Well, you see, twenty years isn't nineteen, and it's not yet twenty-one'. It was difficult to quarrel with that.

Certainly it seems true that Slavs show a greater propensity for celebrating anniversaries than most others. The millennium of Polish Catholicism in 1966 was prepared in depth by a novena of nine years. John Paul has tried to get the Latin American bishops to emulate this by celebrating a novena in anticipation of 1992, the five hundredth anniversary of the discovery of the new world by Christopher Columbus. He went to Santo Domingo, where Columbus made his first landfall, in October 1984 to start the novena rolling.

1985 was also the commemoration of 1100 years of SS Cyril and Methodius, the two Greek brothers from Salonika who evangelized the Slav peoples and even reached the Vislani tribe in southern Poland. Unable to visit the tomb of Methodius in Velehrad in Czechoslovakia, John Paul turned the speech he would have given there into an encyclical letter, *Slavorum Apostoli* ('Apostles of the Slavs', dated 2 June 1985). Then 1988 will be the millennium of Christianity in the Ukraine and Russia – a celebration to which Pope John Paul would dearly love to be invited. But these are the really big anniversaries that permit a reinterpretation of history, provide a reminder of 'the rock from which we are hewn' (Isaiah 51:1), and present an embarrassing challenge to Communist regimes who try to turn them into 'cultural' events drained of all religious import. Twenty years does not seem to be in quite the same league.

Tomko endeavoured to answer this difficulty:

> Twenty years is not a long period for measuring an event of such historic importance as the Council. Yet the acceleration of the pace of life resulting from the rapidity of the changes characteristic of our age necessitates a continual re-examination and a vigilant realization of the letter and spirit of the Council.

Perhaps he might have tried to describe some of the unforeseen changes since 1965 which give the description of the 'signs of the times' in *Gaudium et Spes* a slightly faded air: the multiplication of weapons of destruction, and the threat of their extension into space;

the rise of oil prices, with its consequences for North–South relations; unemployment in the developed world, famine in Africa, genocide and refugees in South-east Asia; a growing women's movement (described as 'a ticking time-bomb in the Church'); a desperate need to prepare future ministers of the Church who would not only be male and celibate.

Tomko loftily soared above all these changes. Instead, this sociologist turned canonist essayed a poetic metaphor:

> The Synod is like a lens or prism which receives and concentrates the light of (in this case the Council) and then refracts it and breaks it up into the entire spectrum of shades and colours, placing in relief the individual components of that luminous source.

One is impressed, indeed dazzled, but without quite knowing what the good man is on about. More important was what may be called 'Tomko's last throw', an attempt to define the *collegial* nature of the Synod. Despite the cautious qualifications, he appeared at last to be saying something significant:

> The bishops of the Church, who are all personally present at a Council, participate through their representatives in the Synod of bishops which is thus, in a certain sense, and to a different degree, a type of continuation of the collegial action of the bishops in a Council.

It was rather like extracting a painful tooth. But what mattered was that Tomko had boldly asserted the collegial nature of the Synod against Cardinal Joseph Ratzinger. For Ratzinger held that bishops only enjoyed the *magisterium* either individually when they taught in their dioceses or collectively when they were gathered round the Pope in a Council. Intermediate bodies – episcopal conferences, regional groupings, CELAM (the Latin American Bishops' Conference) synods – had no theological status and no mandate to teach. Tomko disagreed.

The Synod Council, of which Tomko was still (just) Secretary, met in Rome on 14–15 March. Most of its members were elected – three by continent – towards the end of the previous Synod on reconciliation in autumn 1983. These elections represented a popularity contest among this unique peer group. It was the way Cardinal Karol Wojtyla had emerged on the Church's international stage. In 1983 the Americas had elected two Brazilian Franciscans, Cardinals Evaristo Arns of São Paulo and Aloisio Lorscheider of

Fortaleza, and Cardinal Joseph Bernadin of Chicago. Europe had elected Cardinal Roger Etchegaray, then Archbishop of Marseilles but by this time in the Roman Curia as President of Justice and Peace, Cardinal Carlo Maria Martini, Archbishop of Milan, and Cardinal Basil Hume of Westminster.

One thinks naturally of the elected Council of the Synod as a kind of board of management. But this is misleading. In practice it has very little authority since its members do not even automatically attend the Synod they have helped to prepare. Their presence depends on whether they are included in the fifteen per cent of delegates personally invited by the Pope. In March, no one knew who would be on the list. When it was unveiled in October, neither Bernadin nor Martini nor Arns was there. Since Hume and Etchegaray were present under a different title anyway, it seemed not unfair to conclude that the Synod Council was being snubbed.

Very little was divulged about their 14–15 March meeting. It was decided to postpone the ordinary Synod on 'The Vocation and Mission of the Laity in the Church and the World' by one year, so that it will now take place in 1987. This was a commonsense decision, partly dictated by financial considerations. There has to be a limit to Synods. But it also accidentally gave grounds for thinking that the ordinary Synod of 1987 would be much better prepared in consultation with the laity – who were its subject, after all – than this hastily convened Extraordinary Synod of 1985.

The other main business was devising an agenda for the end-of-the-year fixture. In the nature of things, the questions raised were liable to be fairly general, permitting both the critics and the partisans of the Council to have their say. Here are the four questions put to each of the 104 episcopal conferences:

1. What has been done to make the Council *known, faithfully accepted*, and *put into practice*?

2. What *benefits* have followed from the Council in the actual life of your Church?

3. Are there any *errors* or *abuses* in the interpretation and application of Vatican II which may have crept in? What has been done or should be done to correct them?

4. What have been the *difficulties* in putting the Council into practice (including those caused by new demands arising from changes in historical circumstances)? What should be laid down after the extraordinary meeting to encourage *further progress*

according to the letter and spirit of Vatican II? (italics in the original)

These questions, vague as they were, represented a compromise in the Synod Council. Question 3 about errors and abuses was put in for Ratzinger, who is professionally concerned with detecting and eradicating them. On the other hand, Basil Hume preferred to stress the importance of question 4 which underlined the continuing implementation of the Council as well as rejecting Ratzinger's distinction between the 'letter' (good) and the 'spirit' (which had become an anti-spirit). Hume also noted that 'the four major questions have been deliberately left open and general so as to allow freedom of response'.

'Freedom of response': there would have been no point in making this remark unless it had been under threat. Hume emerged from this 14–15 March meeting determined to save the Council and the Extraordinary Synod. He detected a lack or at least a limpness of leadership. The fundamental weakness of the Ratzinger case was that the Prefect of the Congregation for the Doctrine of the Faith spoke only in the light of reports crossing his desk – and they were mostly complaints and grumbles. Ratzinger's only constituency was the sad company of those who saw denouncing their fellow Catholics as an important Christian duty.

Diocesan bishops, on the other hand, could tackle these questions in the light of the evidence they had already collected about the impact of Vatican II. For they were not starting from scratch. There had been an ongoing assessment almost everywhere. They had already consulted the faithful. Thus the English and Welsh bishops had assessed the response to Vatican II both before and after the National Pastoral Conference of May 1980, and it was positive. This was not guesswork, but hard sociological fact. Other episcopal conferences, such as the Canadian, found themselves obliged to study the impact of the Council when faced with the prospect of a papal visit. Again, the response was positive. So the general trend in the Church went clean counter to the Roman Curia's preoccupation with the 'errors' and 'abuses' mentioned in question 3. It became a matter of some urgency to know who would prepare the Synod and who would write its script. For the time being, no one knew the answer.

However, before any serious consultation could get under way, there was a most disconcerting event. Two weeks after the meeting of the Synod Council a letter was despatched from the Secretariat officially convoking the Extraordinary Synod. It contained the four questions already agreed upon, but then added nine more questions from some mysterious and anonymous source. On receiving this letter, certain members of the Synod Council are reliably reported to have 'hit the roof'.

There were good reasons for distress and alarm. For while it might just have been possible usefully to discuss four questions in ten days, one could certainly not discuss thirteen in so short a time. So whoever framed these questions did not expect serious consultation before the Synod or serious debate at it. To add impertinence to injury, the questions were said to come from 'the Synod Secretariat of the Holy See' – a curious and utterly novel title for a body which is supposed to defend the interest of the bishops, whose Synod it is. And there was the customary touch of farce: the letter was dated 1 April 1985. Most Europeans keep some form of April fool's day.

But this was no leg-pull. The additional questions clearly aimed at comprehensive coverage of all sixteen Council documets. Here they are:

1. How has the constitution *Dei Verbum* been understood and applied to make divine revelation and Holy Scripture more widely known by the faithful and more integrated into their lives (Scripture–Tradition–*Magisterium*, exegesis, sound translations, regular reading, biblical apostolate, pastoral usage, etc.)?

2. Has the double aspect of the mystery of the Church been rightly understood and translated into real life – that is, the Church as communion, and the Church as hierarchical institution? Can the Church's tasks of sanctification and service be clearly seen in the Church's own life (see *Lumen Gentium*)?

3. Has the Council's doctrine on the universal Church and the particular church been rightly understood? Have internal relationships been established in the Church in a spirit of genuine collegiality and communion; especially with regard to the Supreme Pontiff, the Holy See, the bishops; and also relations between bishops, priests, religious, lay people, councils, etc. (see *Lumen Gentium, Orientalium Ecclesiarum, Christus Dominus, Apostolicam Actuositatem*, etc.).

4. Is there a correct notion of liturgy and correct liturgical practice in the genuine spirit of Vatican II (see *Sacrosanctum Concilium*)?

5. What ought to be done to make effective the provisions and hopes of Vatican II about priests and religious, particularly about their training, and also about the Catholic formation of youth (see *Optatam Totius, Perfectae Caritatis, Gravissimum Educationis*)?

6. What is to be done, and how, in carrying out catechesis and moral teaching and specifically in so far as this touches on formation of consciences (Church's *magisterium* and moral theology, norms and conscience, modern questions in medical-social ethics, the moral order in sexual matters, etc.)?

7. What have been the positive results of Vatican II with regard to the proclamation of the Gospel and the encouragement of a 'missionary' spirit (see *Ad Gentes*)?

8. What progress has been made in ecumenism and in dialogue with non-Christian religious and non-believers (see *Unitatis Redintegratio, Nostra Aetate*, etc.)?

9. Is the Church's task with regard to the world and temporal affairs understood and carried out in accordance with the teachings of Vatican II (see *Gaudium et Spes, Inter Mirifica*)?

'This is an agenda', remarked one perspiring bishop, 'for the next twenty Synods or even another Council. Just look at question 6 – how long would it take to deal with test-tube babies and the reception of *Humanae Vitae*?' He was partly consoled by discovering that these questions were marked 'optional'. They were only meant to help. But they revealed a very odd and in one case pre-conciliary outlook: question 8 lumped together other Christians, non-Christians and unbelievers in most insulting fashion. To overlook what Christians already have in common is to travesty one of the most important achievements of the Council. Question 4 was also puzzling in that it had been already adequately dealt with at the October 1984 meeting of the Congregation for Divine Worship.

Apart from hitting the roof, what was in practice to be done? One of the most interesting answers came from Cardinal Carlo Maria Martini, Archbishop of Milan, in a position-paper designed to offer guidance to the Italian Episcopal Conference (CEI) in their perplexity. Martini was the first Jesuit to be a residential bishop in Italy since St Robert Bellarmine in the seventeenth century. He is widely tipped by Italian journalists as a likely future pope. For those who like to scrutinize the entrails Martini gave the retreat to Paul VI and the Roman Curia in Lent 1978, following in the footsteps of Karol Wojtyla who gave it in 1976. And already in this century two popes have come from the ancient and prestigious see of St Ambrose. Rector of the Biblicum and the Gregorian University before his surprise appointment to Milan in 1979, he is certainly the best biblical scholar in the college of cardinals, and has a mind of great penetration and clarity. That is why his position-paper made the rounds of the European bishops. It helped other floundering episcopal conferences to see clearly where they were going.

Working from the scanty documentation available, Martini made a number of methodological points. To avoid rambling incoherently over the entire field, he thought it would be best to concentrate on the mystery of the Church as 'the sacrament of salvation for the whole world'. This was the 'ecclesiological hinge' (*cardo ecclesiologicus*) on which the whole Synod would turn. It would permit a debate on the implementation of the two most fundamental texts of the Council, *Lumen Gentium*, on the nature of the Church, and *Gaudium et Spes*, on the Church in the modern world.

If one concentrated on the Church as sacrament, other alluring topics that had already been or were to be dealt with by other Synods could be set aside. Thus there was no need to deal with the priestly ministry (1971), justice in the world (1971), evangelization (1974), catechesis (1977), the Christian family (1980), the place of the laity in the Church and the world (1987).

Having clearly staked out the ground, Martini sagely remarked that the more clearly defined the Synod agenda, the better episcopal conferences would be able to prepare for it. On the four plus nine questions, he did not hit the roof, but merely expressed his puzzlement:

> It is of course possible to attempt to answer all the questions and so to review every conciliar document and see how it has been applied in our situation with its negative and positive aspects. But then I ask: even if we succeeded in performing this task exhaustively, would it really be of the slightest use for so short a Synod? For I simply do not see how we could deal with all these matters.

In the preliminary texts Martini detected a simple threefold scheme:

1. *obtenta beneficia*: the progress achieved through the Council, the benefits it brought;
2. *defectus et difficultates*: weaknesses and difficulties (which became

in the version of the English and Welsh bishops 'difficulties and failures');

3. *nova incepta*: proposals or suggestions for the further implementation of the Council.

It was important to include 'proposals and suggestions', wrote Martini, because otherwise the Synod could degenerate into 'a merely formal celebration' or (one might add) an acrimonious squabble about the past.

This was a confidential document and it did its work in private. Cardinal Basil Hume decided to go public. He chose 23 April, St George's Day, to give a press conference in Paris. It was a good day to be dragon-slaying. A permanent invitation to talk to Catholic journalists in Paris had been on the table ever since he became Archbishop of Westminster in 1976. He was now invited by Alain Woodrow of *Le Monde* who within six months lost his post as religious affairs correspondent and was transferred to the comparative backwater of television criticism. Hume at last accepted the invitation in April 1985 because he judged his hour had come. He needed to mount his white charger and do battle. He sought to save the Extraordinary Synod from pessimism and catastrophe-thinking. His mother is French and he speaks the language well. A public relations void had been created by the departure of Tomko and the running-in of his replacement, Archbishop Jan Schotte, a Belgian and member of the Scheutist Order. So by going to Paris Hume seized the initiative.

It was not difficult. He assured the French journalists that the Synod would 'not put the clock back' (and this impossibly silly metaphor died the death). Hume intimated that it was not so much that the Council had failed as that we had failed the Council. Blame was distributed fairly widely:

> We have not yet accepted the changes of attitude and practice that are demanded of us, whether we be laity or ordained ministers. We still lack adequate structures and procedures for the exercise of collegiality in the Church, and the proper consultation of every part of the Church.

But was not that the situation the Synod was founded to remedy? It was, but it had not worked out that way. So Hume was trying to breathe some life into the Synod, and make it a forum really dedicated to inner-Church dialogue. He looked beyond the Extraordinary Synod of 1985 to the 1987 Synod on the laity. 'The two themes dovetail in beautifully', he said. But was Hume, as President of the Council of European Bishops' Conferences, made welcome in Paris?

Cardinals do not encroach on each other's patch without securing permission; and in fact Hume was met at the airport by Jean Vilnet, Bishop of Lille, President of the French Episcopal Conference, and he called on Cardinal Jean-Marie Lustiger after lunch. But Lustiger, a convert from Judaism with a Polish family background, had already expounded the official line: the Council was a spiritual event that could not be interpreted in political categories. In an interview with Jean Boudarias in the notoriously conservative *Le Figaro*, Lustiger said:

> The Council was depicted as a battle between the forces of darkness and light. The light was naturally on our side, and of course it had to triumph through the innovative French and German theologians. The forces of darkness were represented by the Curia, those bishops reputed to be 'conservative' and so on. Many people followed the conciliar debates through leaks and indiscretions which tended to reinforce this impression. (*Le Figaro*, 20 February 1985)

Neither Lustiger nor Hume was at the Council. But Hume had a better grasp of history (he studied it at Oxford) and a fuller understanding of the dynamics of the Council. One cannot pretend that there were no clashes at all, that the political dimension was entirely absent or that stories of conflicts were based on tainted sources. Lustiger's attempt to sanitize the Council resembles that of Pope John Paul. Alas, it does not work.

There was another difference between Hume and Lustiger. Hume was made a cardinal by Pope Paul VI in 1976, and therefore did not have to feel personally indebted to Pope John Paul II. Lustiger was named Bishop of Orléans in December 1979 and translated to Paris in January 1981, a rapid rise, owing everything to the personal intervention of the Pope. Furthermore, Lustiger was one of the few French bishops who were unwilling to defend their national catechism, *Pierres Vivantes*, against the attacks launched on it by Cardinal Ratzinger in January 1983. For these various reasons, there would be no Westminster–Paris axis to save the Synod.

Back in London, Cardinal Hume repeated what he had said in Paris and invited everyone – bishops, consultative bodies, individuals – to contribute their thoughts. The invitation was precisely phrased, its scope was broadened to look beyond this particular event, and Martini's emphasis on the life of the Church 'in itself' (*ad intra*) and in relation to the world (*ad extra*) was echoed:

Just as the principal focus of the Council twenty years ago was the nature and life of the Church, so it is suggested that the main concern of the Extraordinary Synod should be with the Church's internal life and external mission. This study may also prove of considerable importance to the part which is now asked of our Church in the proposed Inter-Church Programme of Study, Prayer and Discussion, 1985–7, already announced.

But time was short. This document, the product of the Low Week meeting of the English and Welsh bishops, was dated 25 April 1985. Replies would have to be in by 10 June. One understood later the reason for this hustle: they wanted to publish their response to the questions before the Vatican could stop them.

The European bishops were the first to react because they were closest to the action and grasped its significance. How much concertation there was between them is hardly a matter for conjecture; undoubtedly the Council of European Bishops' Conferences (CCEE), of which Cardinal Hume is President, played an important role. Documents were exchanged. Theologians were consulted. For the previous three years they had been meeting to discuss the topic of 'evangelization in a secularized continent'. They had been groping towards some sophisticated answers. The debate could not be reduced to the simplistic question: are you for or against the Council? It had become rather: how can we develop the logic of the Council still further?

But they were only twenty-five episcopal conferences out of 104 (and they included the East Europeans). Elsewhere in the world, an abstract debate about the fruits of Vatican II did not seem the most pressing of questions. The Brazilians, for example, with over three hundred members by far the largest third-world episcopal conference, received the four plus nine questions almost at the same time as the letter from American Fr John Vaughn, Minister General of the Friars Minor, concerning the fate of Fr Leonardo Boff.

Dated 26 April 1985, and of course highly confidential, it drew the disciplinary consequences of Cardinal Joseph Ratzinger's public letter of 11 February. It said that Boff could teach only members of his own order – previously over a hundred or so lay people and others had been attending his lectures in Petropolis. He was forbidden to appear on TV or speak on the radio or publish articles – as he had done regularly on a weekly basis for many years. He was sacked from his post as editor of the leading Brazilian theological review (*Revista Eclesiástica Brasileira*). He was not allowed to travel: in particular, he must not go to the *Concilium* committee meeting scheduled for Einsiedeln in Switzerland at the end of May. Unlike the three priest ministers in government in Nicaragua, he was not suspended *a divinis* (that is, forbidden to say Mass) or preach, but his sermons were to adhere strictly to the texts of the day and not wander off on to his favourite themes. Boff accepted all this, saying that as a theologian he preferred to 'sing in chorus with the Church rather than do a solo'. But one felt that this was not his last word.

Cardinal Ratzinger blandly explained that this was in no way a 'punitive' measure but rather a kind of 'sabbatical period of reflection'. The Brazilian bishops saw it as an attack not just upon an individual theologian whom they greatly esteemed but upon themselves and upon their pastoral policies as a whole. The two Brazilian members of the Synod Council, Cardinals Arns and Lorscheider, had always defended Boff. They had even accompanied him to Rome for his colloquium on 7 September 1984, thus giving the lie to the notion that Boff had invented a 'popular Church' at odds with the hierarchy. They were the hierarchy and they were in solidarity with Boff. So they were pessimistic about a Synod from which it seemed likely they would be excluded. Lorscheider explained in a private interview how he saw his own role as bishop:

> I'm not the local branch manager of the International Spiritual Bank Inc. I learn as much from my people as they learn from me. They confirm my faith as much as I confirm theirs. When I arrive on horseback or in a jeep, I do not preside all the time. When you ask me what I think, I tell you what their views are.

Despite this, Lorscheider was eventually named as one of the papal nominees for the Synod. But he was counterbalanced by his fellow Brazilian Cardinal Eugenio de Araújo Sales, Archbishop of Rio de Janeiro, the cuckoo in the nest of the Brazilian bishops, sworn foe of liberation theology and the Vatican's principal source of information about the Church in Brazil. For all these reasons the Brazilians did not have high hopes for the Extraordinary Synod.

Meanwhile, Pope John Paul was preparing to visit Holland, Luxembourg and Belgium where he would offer another answer to the question: what do you think of Vatican II?

4

Into the Cockpit of Europe

The Dutch awaited the Extraordinary Synod with some apprehen-- sion. This was because they had already had the experience of a special Synod devoted to themselves. In January 1980 the seven Dutch bishops were summoned to Rome, locked up in a fifteenth-century room in the Vatican and invited to discuss 'the pastoral work of the Church in the Netherlands in the present situation'. Dutch journalists flocked to Rome to cover this important event. But they were not allowed to know what was happening. Pope John Paul explained at a general audience the reasons for this secrecy at a general audience:

> I am sure you will understand that the Church, like all families, at least on certain occasions, needs to have moments of exchange, discussion and decision which take place in intimacy and discretion, to enable the participants to be free and to respect people and situations.

The Dutch journalists, used to open government, found this unconvincing. The idea that the bishops alone made up the family of the Church was offensive and manifestly against both the letter and the spirit of Vatican II. The contrast between the secrecy that shrouded their 1980 special Synod and the openness that had marked the meetings of their Pastoral Council (abolished in 1970) was most striking, all the more since the special Synod undid much of the work of the Pastoral Council.

For these reasons, the Dutch could hardly be expected to look forward to a Synod, whether special, ordinary or extraordinary, with any extravagant hopes. The experience of the Synod in this pontificate was that they had tried to stop many things and started nothing. Vatican II had enthused the Catholic world; the Synods of this pontificate had been merely depressing. This no doubt explained the notable lack of enthusiasm for the papal visit to the Netherlands arranged for 11–15 May 1985. The Dutch rightly guessed the Pope was coming to continue the work of the special Synod of 1980 by propping up the conservative minority in their Church (estimated as Bishop Jan Gijsen of Roermond plus five per cent). The most recent episcopal appointments showed clearly the Pope's intentions: no one would be appointed bishop who had lived in the Netherlands in the last twenty years. So the extraordinary situation was reached in which the whole world was scoured for non-contaminated Dutchmen, and bishops were hauled in from Ethiopia, Louvain and the Salesian Generalate in Rome. It almost seemed that in papal eyes the fact that an episcopal appointment was unpopular proved its wisdom.

But all this had to be deduced from what happened. It was never clearly statted. Most commentators took refuge in airy allusion. Thus Fr Aidan Nichols, an English Dominican teaching at the Angelicum University in Rome, defended Cardinal Ratzinger's pessimistic assessment and bluntly declared: 'The fact of the matter is that in more than one part of the world the Catholic Church is manifestly falling apart' (*The Tablet*, 9 March 1985). He did not disclose where this falling apart was occurring or what its signs were. From South Africa Edmund Hill pointed out that what his brother Dominican called a 'fact' was no more than an opinion – 'it is Fr Aidan's judgement, which he utters without referring to any of the facts or events on which he bases it' (*The Tablet*, 30 March 1985).

However, the Church in the Netherlands is not without self-knowledge. It sometimes admits that it is falling apart. The collapse can be measured by any of the indicators that sociologists would normally use in testing the health of an institution. Thus the number of priests has declined dramatically, and no new ones are coming forward. Religious life, once flourishing, is now mostly a matter of caring for a growing number of senior citizens who will not be replaced. Parish life has slumped, and only about twenty per cent of Dutch Catholics go to Mass. So one could go on with the gloomy statistics of collapse.

But it would not actually prove anything. The figures tell a story of decline, but they do not say what has caused it. The Dutch bishops in their report to the Synod emphasize that one must not confuse *post hoc* with *propter hoc*: what happened after the Council was not necessarily the result of the Council. The Church reflected the pressures and movements of the world. 'Secularization', whatever it meant, was not a wholly negative phenomenon: the end of Christendom and 'sociological Catholicism' might rightly be deplored, but it meant that the faithful remnant were more deeply committed and had a more mature faith. The decline in religious and priestly vocations had enormously stimulated lay ministries. And if Mass attendance was made the norm, then the Dutch twenty per cent was as good as France and better than Italy about which no one ever seemed to agonize or write depressing articles. So the Dutch felt picked upon and grievously misunderstood.

The Polish misunderstanding of Holland was long-standing. In their proposals for the agenda of Vatican II, the Dutch bishops had outlined in 1960 a theology of the Church which was unwelcome to the Roman Curia and yet eventually triumphed. The emphasis of *Lumen Gentium* on the Church as the People of God, on the collegiality of the bishops and on the legitimate autonomy of the local church, owed a lot to the Dutch, although they were not of course alone (see Michel van der Plas, *Brieven an Paus Joannes*, 1984). There was no equivalent Polish contribution to the *ecclesiological* thinking of the Council. And the slowness with which the Council was implemented in Poland (described in chapter 2) contrasted with the heady sense of liberation experienced by the Dutch church. So the two local churches were fated to misunderstand each other. That would not have mattered so long as neither a Dutchman nor a Pole was Pope. Ironically enough, the last non-Italian Pope, Adrian VI, was Dutch, and John Paul visited his house in Utrecht. Adrian died in 1523 after a reign of little over a year, poisoned, it was said, by his physician, to whom the grateful Roman populace erected a monument: for Adrian was a reformer.

Just before the papal visit to Holland, the Dutch church invited parties of foreign journalists to the Netherlands to help them understand this small country (fifteen millions) where Catholics used to be a persecuted minority. It was a pity that Pope John Paul or his entourage could not have had such an experience: after all, one needs to listen before one can confidently pronounce. There was an astonishing consistency in the Dutch account of themselves. Bishops, priests, learned Dominicans, pastoral workers, ordinary believers, government ministers, lay theologians, all said exactly the same thing. It was as if they had been coached.

They began their account of the state of the Church by drawing attention to the Dutch 'national character'. Their 'national character' makes them argumentative and outspoken. They say what they think. They hate secrecy. They love democracy and freedom. They will not allow Opus Dei in their midst, having fought Spanish tyrants in the past. 'Dutchness', said Bishop Ronald Philippe Bär osb of Rotterdam, led people not only to disregard rules they thought made no sense, but to ask that the rule be changed. While Catholics round the world paid lip-service to *Humanae Vitae* as expressing an 'ideal', that, alas, not everyone could reach all at once, the Dutch roundly declared that it was simply mistaken.

'Dutchness' also entailed 'pragmatism' and 'realism'. Both these terms were used by Bishop Bär to explain why the 1980 special Synod had been largely ineffectual: its forty-six propositions did not work on the ground. It was not 'received'. Bishop Bär did not necessarily approve of what he was describing: he was merely explaining the grounds for the misunderstanding of Holland. He has an interesting personal story: he began life as a Calvinist, and then thought of joining the Old Catholics who broke away from Rome in the eighteenth century. The Old Catholic Bishop of Utrecht chivalrously pointed out that there were only 10,000 Dutch Old Catholics and therefore they did not really count for much. He advised the young Philippe Bär to join the Church of Rome. Ditching his fiancée, he entered the Benedictine Abbey of Chevetogne in Belgium (and thus remained 'uncontaminated').

I have developed this idea of 'national character' because the Dutch themselves insisted upon it as the key to their situation. But pushed too far it could be a dangerously 'racist' concept. The truth it contains could probably be better expressed by talking of a national culture. People who have a shared historical experience and a shared language tend to think in the same way. They take the same values for granted. There is a tacit and unspoken agreement among them about what really matters. They may never really know in what this cultural *consensus* consists. It may take an outsider to notice it, but outsiders are resented on the grounds that they simply do not understand. They have not shared in the cultural conversation. They are like people joining a dinner party at 11 p.m. by which time the guests have established much common ground and dismissed some questions as probably unanswerable. Pope John Paul II on his pastoral visit to Poland joined in the cultural conversation at about 11.30 p.m. and inevitably cut clean across it.

This was graphically illustrated on Thursday 8 May 1985 when, two days before the Pope arrived, ten thousand Dutch Catholics gathered in a large tent at Malieveld in The Hague to present what they called 'the other face of the Church'. They feared that what Pope John Paul was going to be allowed to see was a false and heavily made-up face. In fact they need not have worried. Dutch Catholicism is like Brighton rock: it goes all the way down. The

Church that officially introduced itself to the Pope in the Jaarbeurs (Trade Fair building) in Utrecht the following Sunday was recognizably the same as that manifested in The Hague. The only difference was that some of the 'stars' such as Edward Schillebeeckx and Catharina Halkes, the first professor of women's theology at the Catholic University of Nijmegen, were in The Hague but preferred to absent themselves from the Jaarbeurs in Utrecht.

What became apparent was that the real difference between Holland and the Vatican cannot be reduced to a quarrel over particular questions such as contraception or homosexuality. To say that is to trivialize the issue. The difference lies in two contrasting attitudes towards the Church. The Dutch have different expectations about the Church. Or, more simply, they have a different way of 'being Church'. Here is Michel van der Plas, a leading Dutch layman, speaking at Malieveld:

> The Church is not only a Church of saints, she is also, and especially, a Church of sinners. And we are the Church. Often the Church is dishonest, insincere, but we are the Church. The Church still has aspects of power and triumphal features, but we are the Church.
>
> The Church is still too clerical, the Church ignores the value and dignity of women, the Church is too reluctant to admit guilt, the Church is too hard on dissidents, the Church adheres to a too inexorable morality, but we are the Church. *Ecclesia semper reformanda*: the Church is always in need of reform.

This is the profession of faith of a committed 'insider'. He judges himself as harshly as he judges the Church. He sees his own failures as failures of the Church. This passage shows that there is no schismatic intent in the Netherlands – nor has there ever been. These people are not going to 'leave the Church'. That expression has no meaning for them. They can no more leave the Church than they can jump out of their skins.

Moreover, the Dutch claim that what they have done is a legitimate and wholly proper development of Vatican II. If they are now to be bullied and harried, it is for fidelity to the spirit of Vatican II. As they see it, to reproach them with unorthodoxy is merely a pretext for attacking Vatican II. So the commemoration of twenty years after Vatican II would mean one thing in Holland and another in the mind of Pope John Paul II. The May visit to Holland would dramatize this impasse. That is why it figures in this story.

There is not much else to report about the papal visit to the Netherlands. The Pope and the Dutch were on different wavelengths. They optimistically hoped that he had come to listen, but as Cardinal Adriaan Simonis, the primate, admitted on the eve of the visit, 'there is no time for dialogue'. Even the fact that John Paul had mastered the language sufficiently to read out all his speeches in Dutch helped less than might have been thought; for the Dutch are good linguists and felt that the time spent on learning Dutch could have been devoted to understanding the way their minds worked.

On the other hand, the Dutch were permitted to glimpse how John Paul's mind worked. His very first sermon in the magnificently renovated Gothic basilica of Den Bosch showed that he would give the most restrictive interpretation of Vatican II. It was to Den Bosch that he had just appointed Bishop Jan Ter Schure, against the wishes of all the deans. The Bishop of Den Bosch during the Council was Wilhelmus Bekkers, an immensely popular man, known to the whole country as 'the Pope John of the Netherlands'. Ter Schure was mouse-like in comparison. Bekkers' emphasis on 'The Church on the Way' summed up the questing and open-minded attitude of the Dutch church in the conciliar period; it had neither pat formulas nor neat solutions to offer, but it could accompany people on a journey to the heart of their problems and the heart of the Gospel.

This language is now out of fashion. In Den Bosch John Paul tried to 'recuperate' the heritage of Bishop Bekker:

I greet all of you here today, and would like to express my joy at being here among you, together with you, the People of God. This is what the second Vatican Council called the Church . . . I am happy that I have been able to take part with you in the procession through the streets of Den Bosch.

The speech was, of course, written in advance. There had been hardly anyone in the streets of Den Bosch. The Pope plunged bravely on:

This was a symbol of the spiritual journey which God's people must make. We are journeying together towards our Father's house. My presence here among you is a symbol of the unity of the Dutch church with the Church of Rome and consequently with the universal Church. We are a pilgrim people. The second

43

Vatican Council spoke of the People of God 'going forward in this present world in search of a future and abiding city'.

So far, it might be said, John Paul was echoing chapter 2 of *Lumen Gentium* which is devoted to 'the People of God'. But then he moved on to chapter 3 on 'the hierarchical structure of the Church with special reference to the episcopate'. He believes that the Dutch church has assimilated chapter 2 of *Lumen Gentium* but needed reminding of chapter 3. So at this point he introduced his defence of Ter Schure's appointment. It was a truly extraordinary scene. Never before has a Pope publicly defended an episcopal appointment, and never before has the new bishop been sitting sheepishly just a few feet away while the Pope explained the reasons for his unpopularity.

> I know that you have been going through a difficult time in recent weeks. The recent appointments of bishops have deeply offended some of you who are wondering about the reason for these tensions.
> I should like to say in all sincerity that the Pope attempts to understand the life of the local church in the appointment of every bishop. He gathers information and takes advice in accordance with ecclesiastical law and custom. You will understand that opinions are sometimes divided. In the last analysis, the Pope has to take the decisions. (Must he explain his choice? Discretion does not permit him to do so.)
> Believe me, brothers and sisters, this suffering on account of the Church grieves me. But be convinced that I have truly listened, considered carefully, and prayed. And I appointed the person whom I thought before God the most suitable for this office. (11 May 1985, in St John's Cathedral, s'Hertogenbosch; the two sentences in brackets were omitted in delivery.)

Yet despite this appeal, the Dutch remained unconvinced. It was difficult to believe that the Pope had time to take such an intensely personal interest in every diocese of the world; and they suspected that the 'discretion' which made him withhold an explanation was a cover for a desire to restore order and discipline in the Netherlands. Only in that sense could Ter Schure be considered 'the most suitable' candidate for this office. It would perhaps have been better to have said so frankly. The Dutch would have respected that.

But this controversy about the new Bishop of Den Bosch raised much wider questions, and they were crucial to the forthcoming

Synod. What is, or should be, the relationship of the local church and the universal Church? How much legitimate autonomy has a local church and its episcopal conference? How far is it free to interpret or develop Vatican II in the light of its own needs?

One of the sharpest differences of opinion was on the question of ministry. Hardly any priests are being ordained in Holland. In 1984 the figure was seven for Roermond (Gijsen's diocese in the southeast) and six for the remaining six dioceses. Haarlem had none. Meanwhile, the number of 'pastoral workers', in effect unordained curates, is increasing. They number 324, of whom about a third are women. In 1980 the special Synod expressed its fear that the 'pastoral workers' were in danger of becoming 'a parallel clergy which would appear as an alternative to the priesthood and the diaconate'. This is a real threat as can be seen by looking at the five theological colleges of the Netherlands. They are full. But the young men want to be 'pastoral workers' rather than priests because of the requirement of celibacy, and the young women have to be 'pastoral workers' because the priesthood is not open to them.

Edward Schillebeeckx has developed his theology of ministry on the basis of the actual situation in Holland. As priests grow older and vanish altogether, the pastoral workers, who are already running the parishes, will have to be ordained, whether they are married or female. Schillebeeckx then appeals to history to show that the Church need never lack priests, for it has always given itself the ministers it required (see *The Church with a Human Face. A New and Expanded Theology of Ministry*, 1985). The ideas in this book had already been under fire from the Congregation for the Doctrine of Faith. But Schillebeeckx had shown that he did not hold the view attributed to him that ministry comes wholly 'from below' (from the Christian people) rather than 'from above' (from the ordaining bishop); and so he escaped censure – this time round. But he remained the invisible interlocutor on Sunday 12 May when John Paul addressed what was tactfully called 'a meeting of parish priests with their helpers'. It included most of the 'pastoral workers' besides many others engaged in catechetical, liturgical, missionary or charitable ministries.

This time the Dutch were happy with John Paul's speech. He implicitly commended 'pastoral workers' (along with all the rest): 'I am here to urge you to continue with your work'. That was progress, for Bishop Gijsen will not allow 'pastoral workers' in his diocese at all. However, there was as usual a *caveat*. John Paul quoted his Maundy Thursday 1979 letter to priests which recalls the conciliar idea that there is an 'essential distinction and not merely a difference of degree' between the priestly ministry and other ministries. So there is not some point on the horizon where the general priesthood of all the baptized will merge into that of the ordained priestly ministry. Then he quoted resolution 33 of the special Synod of the Dutch church which welcomes pastoral workers provided they do not usurp the priestly role. Here is how they are described:

> Lay persons play a great part in the pastoral life of the Church. The task which they are allotted by the bishop is an invitation to co-operate closely with priests and deacons in preaching the Word of God, being witnesses to the message of Christ and inculcating Gospel values at all levels of society. By virtue of suitable theological and pastoral training they will deepen a sense of their own mission, in which as lay people they are directly connected with the pastoral mission of the Church. They will refuse to be simply church officials or to take on tasks that are the prerogative of the priests and deacons.

It is very difficult to 'cash' these remarks. They encourage 'pastoral workers' up to a point. They make it clear that they cannot hear confessions or celebrate the Eucharist. But they do not say what should happen when there are no more ordained priests. That is a situation the Pope simply refuses to envisage. By refusing it, he hopes to 'encourage vocations'.

On the other hand John Paul was clear and scathing about so-called 'base communities' (actually more usually called 'critical communities' in Holland) where sometimes laicized priests or the non-ordained celebrate the Eucharist:

> They bear witness to positive values wherever their members try simply and sincerely to give form to the Gospel in their everyday lives. But the danger is that these communities then regard themselves as the only form of churchliness. They run the risk of splitting off into small groups and setting themselves against what they call 'the institutional Church'.

But even here there was a recognition, however grudging, of ambivalence.

So what happened in Holland? Was it a case of the irresistible force meeting the immovable obstacle? Would Dutch stubbornness be able to hold out against Polish determination? The Pope clearly believed that it was his duty to go to Holland and reverse an historical trend. He would try to roll back the tide of secularization. On arrival he remarked that 'the vitality of a local church increases or is revived to the extent that they do not become shut up in themselves and do not distance themselves from the centre of the Church's unity' (11 May, Eindhoven airport). Evidently he believed that the Dutch church had succumbed to both these temptations.

But it is far from certain that one can reverse historical trends merely by making speeches denouncing them. From this point of view, one of the most significant statements came from Cardinal Adriaan Simonis who explained to Pope John Paul, just before he left, why the special Synod of 1980 had been ineffectual:

> We are doing our utmost to implement the decisions of the Synod. But it is taking longer than we expected. Reality teaches us that, measured in human terms, the Holy Spirit does not always work in the same way and at the same time among the shepherds and large sections of the flock. (14 May 1985: meeting with the episcopal conference)

It has to be admitted that Simonis does not have a very good reputation with the progressive Dutch Catholics who gathered in Malieveld. Yet here he was admitting in the presence of the Pope the most fundamental principle of the entire Dutch experiment: the Holy Spirit is present and at work in the whole Church, and not just in the bishops. But that was precisely the question at issue in the Extraordinary Synod. It would be an exercise in discerning where the Holy Spirit is now.

The visit to Belgium was happier and duller. After the hailstorms in Holland the sun came out and so did the crowds. The magnificent baroque squares of Flanders were designed for a triumphant royal progress. Belgium, after all, is a 'Catholic country'. Moreover, although without firsthand experience of Holland, Pope John Paul knew Belgium and the Belgians well: he lived at the Belgian College in Rome in 1946–8. He shared in their national feasts and celebrated their heroes: Cardinal Désiré Mercier, promoter of the Malines conversations between Anglicans and Catholics in the 1920s; Dom Lambert Beauduin OSB, founder of the ecumenical Abbey of Chevetogne; and Cardinal Joseph Cardijn who founded the Young Christian Workers and inspired their see-judge-act approach to social and industrial problems. They were all duly evoked. John Paul felt at home in Belgium.

Yet paradoxically it was in Belgium that he chose to deliver an attack of quite exceptional ferocity on theologians. In Holland he had ignored them. But now, addressing the Belgian bishops in Malines and recalling their last *ad limina* visit, he said:

> In Rome I asked you to be yourselves bishop-theologians in the field, in close co-operation with the professional theologians who methodically explore the content of the faith, without creating a parallel *magisterium*, for the bishops teach by virtue of the legitimate *magisterium* (cf. Pius XII, *Acta Apostolica Sedis*, 1954, pp. 314–15).
>
> There is but one *magisterium*, entrusted to the apostles united to Peter and to their successors. With these theologians, encourage the understanding of the faith. There are errors to be pointed out by name, there are renewed propositions of the faith to be deepened.

What *had* Belgian theologians been up to? Now that there are two theology faculties – one at Leuven for the Flemings and the other at Louvain for the Walloons – the scope for complaint was wide. Leuven gave an honorary degree to the El Salvadorian liberation theologian, Jon Sobrino sj. Cardinal Godfried Danneels, Archbishop of Malines-Brussels, was a contemporary of Gustavo Gutierrez at Louvain and admires his work. Moreover, Danneels had been to Peru in autumn 1984, met Gutierrez and Leonardo Boff and did not disguise his view that the Instruction 'On certain forms of liberation theology' was wholly inadequate. 'If I were in Latin America', he said, 'I would no doubt be with the liberation theologians for they are renewing the Church from the base upwards. To discourage them would be a catastrophe.'

The Pope must have had precise theologians in view for he said that 'there are errors to be pointed out by name'. The Belgian bishops were failing in this respect. The most curious feature of this Malines speech was the quotation from Pius XII in 1954. To have to reach back in the Church's memory to that unhappy year when Pius XII nearly died was a sign of desperation: the whole nature of the working relationship between theologians and bishops had changed since then. For one thing, it was never simply true that there were bishops on the one side, possessing some magical property called the *magisterium*, confronting a rival team of theologians whose aim in life was to undermine or purloin episcopal authority. This is a complete fantasy. For bishops have to get their theological arguments from somewhere, and they get them from theologians. The exaltation of the *magisterium* over theologians really boils down to a preference for one group of theologians over another. Danneels, a former professor at Louvain, was well aware of this. He must have been perturbed by this unwarranted onslaught.

John Paul, however, in this same speech, did 'point out' one error 'by name'. The name of the error was 'secularization'. Perhaps the real reason why theologians were attacked was that they are deemed responsible for not putting up sufficiently strong barriers against 'secularization', and even being infiltrated by it:

> The crisis is important and profound. Today people tend to refuse God in the name of their own humanity. This secularization, which could in itself be but an aspect of the legitimate distinction between temporal and spiritual (cf. *Gaudium et Spes*, no. 36), is grave in that it affects the Church herself, and even priestly and religious life. The second Vatican Council determined the basic principles and means by which the Church has to carry out an appropriate spiritual renewal. But in so far as some have studied, interpreted or applied it badly, this renewal has here and there been a cause of disarray and division, and it has been unable to prevent a religious decline. (18 May 1985; Malines)

Once more, it is not easy to see exactly what John Paul is getting at. The idea seems to be that some Catholics, either individually or collectively, have so eagerly embraced 'the secular meaning of the Gospel' that they have forgotten its Christian meaning. This certainly can happen. But the relevant point here is that this error is traced back to a faulty interpretation of *Gaudium et Spes*.

So the visit to what in the seventeenth and eighteenth centuries was known as 'the cockpit of Europe' clarified the aim of the Extraordinary Synod. There was nothing wrong with the doctrines of the Council *as such*; but it had been badly interpreted. In the Netherlands the emphasis fell on the partial and erroneous reading of *Lumen Gentium*, in Belgium on the misunderstanding of *Gaudium et Spes*. In the mind of the Pope, therefore, the function of the Synod would be to remedy this state of affairs. In the plane on the way back from Belgium, a reporter asked John Paul what would be the content of the Extraordinary Synod. His question was brushed aside with, 'Oh, I leave that sort of thing to Cardinal Ratzinger'.

5

Ratzinger invites Trouble

So Cardinal Joseph Ratzinger, Prefect of the Congregation for the Doctrine of Faith since January 1982, was according to Pope John Paul the man most likely to fix the agenda of the Extraordinary Synod. He had already done so unofficially in an interview given to the Italian magazine *Jesus* (November 1984) in which he pleaded for the 'restoration' of pre-conciliar values. He was no longer talking about the Church 'manifestly falling apart in more than one or two places'. It was the post-conciliar Church as a whole that had 'opened itself indiscriminately to an atheistic and agnostic world'. Who had brought this about? Theologians were the guilty men, especially those who used the catch-phrase 'anonymous Christians' to undermine missionary work or those who flirted with 'the illusory myth that class struggle is an instrument for the creation of the classless society'. Equally harmful were moral theologians (especially in the United States) many of whom 'believe they have to choose between clashing with their society and clashing with their bishops. Many chose the latter course, agreeing to compromise with a secular ethic'. However, bishops were not exempted from this diatribe: they have to be liberated from the bureaucratic stranglehold of the episcopal conference which has neither theological reality nor mandate to teach. It was evident that a Ratzinger-inspired Synod would not have much to celebrate. Its purpose would be to denounce these errors and begin the urgent task of pre-conciliar restoration.

'Do not judge Cardinal Ratzinger on the interview', said his friends, 'wait for the book.' The book *Rapporto sulla Fede* eventually appeared towards the end of May 1985 (translated into English as *The Ratzinger Report*, November 1985). Fr Aidan Nichols assured everyone that the book was selling like hot cakes in Rome. But it was being bought largely by theologians anxious to refute its many slurs on their profession. For the book was even more pessimistic

than the original interview. *The Tablet*'s anonymous reviewer put
his finger on it straightaway:

> The language provides the first and easiest clue to the Cardinal's
> mind-set. After a while I stopped counting the number of times
> words like 'dangers', 'problems', 'risks' and 'crisis' turn up. . . .
> The Cardinal clearly holds that Vatican II was a good thing.
> But he portrays the post-conciliar decades as largely a period of
> 'dissent', 'self-destruction', 'discouragement' and 'decadence', in
> which 'every kind of heretical deviation' has been 'beating at the
> door of authentic faith'. He believes that the 'authentic reception'
> of the Council has not even yet begun. Its documents got 'buried
> under a heap of publications' which were often 'superficial and
> inaccurate'. Here one cannot help recalling that Cardinal Ratz-
> inger himself contributed to a large and widely read commentary
> on Vatican II edited by Herbert Vorgrimler. ('Ratzinger's sad
> book', in *The Tablet*, 13 July 1985)

This threw Ratzinger's defenders into something of a panic. Fr
Aidan Nichols agreed with the reviewer in thinking that it would
have been better to have listed the signs of hope alongside the
evidence of collapse. But he charitably attributes this omission to
overwork; 'One must not lay too many burdens on those who bear
the heat of the day in the Lord's vineyard' ('In support of Ratzinger', *The Tablet*, 28 July 1985). But Ratzinger's pessimism has
deeper roots than that.

The pessimistic opinions he expressed are not uncommon. They
can be seen almost weekly in the correspondence columns of the
Catholic press. Little magazines in almost every country in the
world attack allegedly 'neo-modernist theologians', exempt themselves from the ordinary requirements of charity, practise calumny
on a grand scale and show a fine disregard for the laws of libel.
Bodies like Catholics United for the Faith (CUF) in the United
States encourage their members to write to the Vatican with horror
stories denouncing local theologians, catechists, sisters, bishops.
Ratzinger admits in his book that much of his knowledge of the
international scene comes from these reports. He was never a great
traveller. Yet five minutes in a Latin American bookstore permit
him to generalize: 'There, and not only there, I noticed that popular
manuals of psychoanalysis had taken the place of spiritual treatises;
theology had given way to psychology'. I doubt if this bookshop
could be named. Ratzinger and his informers live in a world of self-
generated anxiety.

None of this would matter if Joseph Ratzinger were merely one theologian among others. But as Prefect of the CDF the relationship with his peer group has totally changed. He now has power to silence theologians, remove them from their teaching posts, break their careers, deprive them of the title 'Catholic theologian', and quash their aspirations. But of course what he says in his interview does not have any of these effects. He is not wearing the biretta of Prefect of the CDF. He is merely expressing his private opinions. This is what Pope John Paul said in the plane on the way back from Africa on 19 August:

> What Cardinal Ratzinger says is his own opinion. He is free to express his own opinion. His opinion corresponds to many events, but it cannot be understood in this [meaning] that the Council, Vatican II, was a negative meaning for the Church – no, on the contrary.

The Pope was speaking in English to Bill Pritchard of the National Catholic News Service. His words were accurately reported. Though rather obscure they mean that Ratzinger's opinions 'do not commit the Holy See'.

Others had already reached this same conclusion for themselves. One could therefore attack Ratzinger's opinions without attacking the Holy See. By giving an interview, Ratzinger did what none of his predecessors had done and made a tactical blunder: he stepped down from his prefectorial podium and put himself on the same level as his fellow theologians. He practically invited them to hit him on the chin. They did so with great zest, not pulling their punches, and accusing him of misrepresentation, superficiality and carelessness. Here is one example:

> Apparently the Cardinal feels competent to answer questions on practically anything related to Church life and affairs. The results include a superficial presentation of the ordination of women that takes no account of the data which led the Pontifical Biblical Commission to say that of itself the New Testament does not decide the matter. To put it mildly, there is some tension between Cardinal Ratzinger's picture of a morality specially revealed to Moses and a morality 'written' in our created human nature. Many would dispute the Cardinal's claim that the 1983 Code of Canon Law is 'perfectly' aligned with the renewal of Vatican II. His response on new difficulties between Anglicans and Orthodox implies an inaccurate picture of the Orthodox discipline on

divorce, remarriage and the sacraments. He repeats the well-worn but unfair accusation that Karl Rahner's thesis about 'anonymous Christians' has helped to undermine evangelization. He absolutizes what some theologians of liberation are saying. . . . Where these theologians hope not only for personal conversion but also for change in economic and political structures, Cardinal Ratzinger portrays them as not calling individuals to conversion at all but being concerned only with changing social structures. (*The Tablet*, 13 July 1985)

In short, one would not buy a used theology manual from this man or entrust him with the theological education of one's daughter. However, Ratzinger does not profit from criticism. In January 1983 he gave a lecture in Paris and another in Lyons attacking *Pierres Vivantes*, the official catechism of the French bishops. Two days later, Gérard Defois, at the time Secretary of the French episcopal conference, arrived in Rome with the French newspapers which, except for *Le Figaro*, were entirely hostile to Ratzinger. Ratzinger did not want to read them. He told Defois: 'I'm like the cellist Rostropovich – I never read the critics'.

One great advantage of the publication of *Rapporto sulla Fede* is that it permits us to see how Ratzinger's mind works and how he arrived at his present position. Vittorio Messori, who conducted the interviews, was anxious to dispel the image of a Grand Inquisitor, a Bavarian bully, a *Panzer* out to crush all theological opposition. Messori met his subject in August 1984 while Ratzinger was on holiday in what the Italians call Alto Adige and the Germans South Tyrol. There in the baroque seminary of Bressanone (Italian) or Brixen (German) the distinguished Cardinal humbly sits down at the table among the aged priests who could afford no other holiday. He accepts the meals provided by the Tyrolese sisters (who know their place). This *mise-en-scène* was meant to banish the impression that Ratzinger is arrogant or inquisitorial. On the contrary, Messori tells us that he laughs heartily and keeps the company entertained with his jokes and witticisms. But this is something of a false trail. Many inquisitors have been personally affable and polite. Edward Schillebeeckx said of his own *colloquium* at the Holy Office in 1980 that the really difficult part was to make social conversation during the coffee-break. Leonardo Boff emerged smiling from his *colloquium* with Ratzinger on 7 September 1984.

As *The Tablet* reviewer remarked, the language reveals the mind-set. Ratzinger always begins amiably and innocently. For example, he denies with some vigour that the categories of 'left' and 'right', 'conservative' and 'liberal' (or 'progressive') can be applied to the life of the Church. For these are notions borrowed from political life that fail to cope with the religious vision of the world which, as Blaise Pascal said, 'is of another order that surpasses all the rest in profundity'. Pascal distinguished the three 'orders' of earth, intellect and charity (*Pensées*, ed. Martin Turnell, no. 585) and said there was no communication between them. A qualitative leap is needed to get from 'earth' to 'intellect' or from 'intellect' to 'charity'.

It is difficult to know what is achieved by this rejection of 'political' language. One can agree that it is improper and inadequate and that it must be irksome to hear oneself repeatedly described as a hidebound conservative or an impenitent right-winger. But we still need some words to describe those who advocate change and those who resist it. Ratzinger himself later admits that in every episcopal conference there are advocates of renewal and cautious men who say 'we mustn't run before we can walk'. That is part of the dynamism of any human gathering. To deny the validity of such language altogether and to escape into 'another order' above the heat and burden of the battle, is usually an alibi for a conservatism that does not wish to be unmasked.

Ratzinger tries to play a similar trick with language when he denies that he may be called a 'pessimist'. To call Christians 'optimistic' or 'pessimistic' is just as misleading as to call them 'conservative' or 'liberal', and for the same reason. Once again, Ratzinger leaps into another dimension. The Christian must be an optimist 'because he makes his own the event which is *par excellence* the basis of optimism – the resurrection of Christ'. This gives him courage 'lucidly to name errors, without closing his eyes or wearing rose-tinted spectacles'. The point seems to be that ultimately the Christian is optimistic because of the resurrection, but that this gives him the right to make harsh judgements in the name of 'realism' about what is actually happening in the Church. Dietrich Bonhoeffer used to distinguish between the realm of the 'ultimate', in which we believe, and the 'penultimate', in which we live. Ratzinger's 'optimism' is therefore confined to his prie-dieu or postponed until some future eschatological event can break in. In the short term, pessimism prevails. Those who do not share it are said to be blind or deluded.

But Ratzinger was not always so negative. The odd thing is that when confronted with his younger conciliar self – the Ratzinger who was adviser to Cardinal Joseph Frings of Cologne during the

Council – he always says that it is the others who have changed. He has remained firm as a rock amid the tempests of mutable opinions. He even quotes a lecture he gave in 1966 to prove the consistency of his pessimism. He is no Johnny-come-lately to pessimism. As long ago as 1966 he perorated:

> Perhaps you expected a more joyful and luminous picture of the Church today. And one could perhaps draw such a picture, on some matters. But it seemed to me important to show the two faces of the event of the Council: we are filled with joy and gratitude, but we also have a call and a task. And it seemed important to point to the danger of a neo-triumphalism among those who denounce most vigorously the triumphalism of the past. So long as the Church is on its earthly pilgrimage, it has no right to glory in itself. This new style of self-glorification could become more insidious than the tiaras and *sedia gestatoria* [or portable papal chair] that, today, inspire smiles rather than pride.

'Triumphalism' – a compound of smugness, arrogance, and prejudice – was what the 'liberals' had accused the 'conservatives' of at the Council. It was castigated along with 'juridicism' and 'clericalism'. Ratzinger had a valid point in 1966. But even so, one wonders whether he should not have used his talents as a renowned Council *peritus* to make its documents better known in Germany. Why did he have to be so negative, so soon? Was it a matter of temperament? Or failed hopes?

Part of the answer lies in his brief experience in 1964 as a board member of the review *Concilium*. Messori asked him, 'in bantering fashion', whether looking back he now regards this collaboration as 'a misfortune', 'a youthful excess' like sowing a few wild oats. Ratzinger replied non-banteringly:

> I have not changed, but they have. From the very first meetings, I made two things clear to my colleagues. *First*, our group should not be sectarian or arrogant, as though we were the new true Church or an alternative *magisterium* with the truth in our pockets. *Secondly*, we have to deal with the authentic letter and spirit of Vatican II, and not with some imaginary Vatican III.

Is he saying that the whole editorial board of *Concilium* fell into these manifest errors and that he had perceived the danger from the outset? Apparently yes.

But what was only hinted at in 1964 became evident (he claims) by 1972: everything that preceded the Council was dismissed as irrelevant, and 'some people' said that Vatican II itself belonged to 'the traditional and clerical period of the Church that had now been superseded'. So it could be discarded. There was a *fuite en avant* – a headlong rush into a not-yet future. I have heard some pretty wild things in my time, especially late at night, but never anything remotely resembling what Ratzinger seems to be attributing to *Concilium*.

What has been said – and repeated in the run-up to the Extraordinary Synod – is that Vatican II does not contain final answers on all matters, that it indicated a direction more than it gave directives, and that on some precise questions it is in need of reworking. The description of the 'signs of the times' in *Gaudium et Spes* is an obvious example: this was how the world looked in 1963–4 when the text was being written. Another example of conciliar inadequacy is the treatment of the laity which oscillates between sending them out into the 'world' and assigning them a ministry within the Church. It was precisely this ambivalence and inadequacy that led Pope John Paul II to ordain 'the Vocational Mission of the Laity in the Church and in the World' as the theme of the next ordinary Synod, now scheduled for 1987. So finding the Council inadequate or incomplete is not the same as rejecting it wholesale. Not for the first time, it seems that Ratzinger caricatures his opponents the better to refute them.

Whether Ratzinger is right or wrong about *Concilium* is a matter of opinion. It is certainly not a dogmatic truth. It does not become any truer with repetition. His distaste for *Concilium* may not be unconnected with the fact that the rival review he supported, *Communio*, never attained the international success of *Concilium*. On the principle of *audiatur altera pars* ('listen to the other side of the question') Ratzinger should ponder carefully what Nicholas Lash, the first Roman Catholic ever to be Norris-Hulse Professor of Theology in Cambridge, said of the *Concilium* board meetings:

I am obliged to be personal. I am the only English member of the central directorate of *Concilium*. We are a mixed bunch, none of us unscarred by the fearfulness and egotism that are the marks of original sin. (But then the same is probably true of some of the officials in the Cardinal's Congregation.) We have all, in our time, said silly things – some sillier than others. Nevertheless I am continually impressed not just by my colleagues' erudition and intelligence, but by their passionate and loyal devotion to the Catholic Church... And yet ever since the Council, and still today, almost every theologian singled out by the Congregation for the Doctrine of the Faith for disciplinary attention or much publicized disapproval, has been drawn from our ranks. ('Catholic theology and the crisis of classicism', in *New Blackfriars*, June 1985, p. 286)

This is not the place to argue the comparative merits of theological studies in German and English-speaking universities. But it is quite clear that in a well-ordered Church Nicholas Lash would be an obvious member of the International Theological Commission (a group of thirty theologians created in response to the Extraordinary Synod of 1969 to make sure that greater theological expertise would be available to the CDF). But that will not happen, for the simple reason that Lash is a 'laicized' priest. It may appear that on the strictly theological level, Lash and Ratzinger are equals, but the truth is that in the end Ratzinger has all the administrative power. This is what makes the sweeping and all-embracing attack on *Concilium* so sinister and menacing for the future.

However, there was no reason to be too gloomy, yet. As Pope John Paul said, Cardinal Ratzinger was merely expressing his own opinions. So others could express their own opinions in reply. Theologians, historians and bishops queued up to refute him. Jean Delumeau, the most famous French church historian, observed that Ratzinger's remark that 'the structures of the Church are unchangeable' was meaningless unless one specified which 'structures' were in view (*Le Monde*, 22 June 1985). The modern practice of the Vatican appointing bishops would have shocked Pope Leo the Great who in 458 wrote to the Bishop of Narbonne: 'No one can become a bishop unless he has been elected by the clergy, asked for by the people, consecrated by the bishops of his province and approved by the Metropolitan'. This made the appointment of unpopular bishops in the Netherlands, discussed in the last chapter, seem even more anomalous.

It was in *Le Monde*, too, that Jacques Gaillot, Bishop of Evreux, observed that Ratzinger did not have the truth in his pocket (the very phrase used by Ratzinger of *Concilium*). He found the book 'profoundly sad'. It did not fit in with his experience on the ground:

Every day I meet Christians who are filled with the freshness of the Gospel. I simply do not see this 'decadence' of which the Cardinal speaks. I wonder indeed if there has ever been a period in history in which the Gospel has been lived out so fully as it is today. I think of those Christians in country parishes, for example, who never separate life and faith and who face up to the gravest contemporary problems with courage and decisiveness. (*Le Monde*, 6 July 1985)

But if historians and pastors had their say, it was theologians who were at this stage most voluble. One cannot follow them over the entire field. It will be useful to concentrate on Ratzinger's critique of episcopal conferences, since it affected the very nature of the Extraordinary Synod which was, precisely, a meeting of presidents of episcopal conferences. If the episcopal conferences had neither theological status nor mandate to teach, as Ratzinger maintained, it followed that a meeting of their presidents would be a tame and uninteresting event.

Ironically enough, one of the best accounts of the theological implications of the setting up of episcopal conferences came from a young theologian writing in *Concilium* in July 1965. Joseph Ratzinger – for it was he – wrote:

Let us dwell for a moment on the bishops' conferences for these seem to offer themselves today as the best means of concrete plurality in unity. They have their prototype in the synodal activity of the regionally different 'colleges' of the ancient Church. They are also a legitimate form of the collegiate structure of the Church. One not infrequently hears the opinion that the bishops' conferences lack all theological basis and could therefore not act in a way that would be binding on an individual bishop. The concept of collegiality, so it is said, could be applied only to the common action of the entire episcopate. Here again we have a case where a one-sided and unhistorical systematization breaks down. The *suprema potestas in universam ecclesiam* which canon 228(1) ascribes to the ecumenical council applies, of course, only to the college of bishops as a whole in union with the Bishop of Rome. But is it always a question of the *suprema potestas* in the Church? Would this not be very sharply reminiscent of the disciples' quarrel about their rank? We would rather say that the concept of collegiality, besides the office of unity which pertains to the Pope, signifies an element of variety and adaptability that basically belongs to the structures of the Church, but may be actuated in many different ways. The collegiality of bishops signifies that there should be in the Church (under and in the unity guaranteed by the primacy) an ordered plurality. The bishops' conferences are, then, one of the possible forms of collegiality that is here partially realized but with a view to the totality. ('The pastoral implications of episcopal collegiality', *Concilium*, no. 1, 1965, p. 30)

Presumably Ratzinger still held these views in 1972 when this *Concilium* article was republished in his book, *Das neue Volk Gottes. Entwürfe zur Ekklesiologie* ('The New People of God. Sketches towards an Ecclesiology'). There was nothing eccentric about them. They represented the consensus of all enlightened theologians at that time.

Ratzinger became Archbishop of Munich in 1977 – but that may be irrelevant. It was after that, however, that he began to change his mind and adopt his present view that the episcopal conference was 'no more than a practical arrangement'. So it no longer had the collegial meaning he assigned to it in 1965. The first time he expressed his new views (to my knowledge) was in January 1983, when the US bishops had been summoned to Rome to have the second draft of their pastoral letter on nuclear weapons put through the sieve. Ratzinger seemed hostile to the draft, not so much because of its contents as of its very existence. For, as he explained: 'A bishops' conference as such does not have a *mandatum docendi* [mandate to teach]. This belongs only to the individual bishops or to the college of bishops with the Pope' (*Origins*, 7 April 1963, p. 692). Moreover, while being presumptuous, the US bishops' draft was also mistaken in its approach: 'It is wrong to propose the teaching of the bishops merely as the basis for debate; the teaching ministry of the bishops means that they lead the people of God and therefore their teaching should not be obscured or reduced to one element among several in a free debate' (ibid.).

So according to Ratzinger there are only two occasions when a bishop may teach validly. The first is when he is in his own diocese. His statements can be binding in conscience. The other is when he gathers with all the bishops of the world around the Pope in a general Council of the universal Church. The second case is bound to be rare: there have been two Councils in the last four centuries. When bishops meet on all other occasions – whether at a national or regional episcopal conference or in the Synod – they have no 'mandate to teach'. There are no intermediate bodies between the individual bishop and a general Council. This theory requires one to believe that while individual bishops may teach away in their dioceses, once they come together the successors of the apostles deposit their *magisterium* (or teaching authority) in the cloakroom with their hats and umbrellas.

However preposterous this may sound, one has to accept that Ratzinger's opinion can be justified if one gives a very strict and merely juridical interpretation of the prefatory note to *Lumen Gentium* (text in Abbott, pp. 97–101). In the 1960s Ratzinger had a different approach. He was trying to answer the objection that the prefatory note would lead to papal arbitrariness for it spoke of the Pope acting 'according to his own discretion' and 'as he chooses'. Ratzinger points out that *moral* as well as juridical factors enter into the equation so that 'among the claims which his office must make on the Pope we must undoubtedly reckon a moral obligation to hear the Church universal. . . Juridically speaking, there is no appeal from the Pope . . . but morally speaking, the Pope may have an obligation to listen' ('Announcements and prefatory notes of explanation', in Herbert Vorgrimler, ed., *Commentary on the Documents of Vatican II*, 1967, vol. I, p. 304). Ratzinger added a comment that he now seems to have forgotten:

> Collegiality . . . is designed to recall the fact that the Church is essentially plural, is a *communio*, that centralization has its limits, and that ecclesiastical acts at national or provincial or diocesan level have their importance – collegiate acts, that is, which do not qualify as *actus stricte collegiales* [strictly collegial acts].

Seen in this light one can welcome the US bishops' pastoral letter and the work of CELAM (the Latin American Bishops' Conference) as *morally collegiate* acts even if they do not meet the strictest of canonical requirements. For the *communio* or *koinonia* which is at the very heart of the Church's unity has moral and spiritual implications that go far beyond what can be juridically set down. Pope John Paul recognizes this by his constant use of the phrase 'affective and effective collegiality'.

It remains to ask why Ratzinger has changed his mind on this fundamental question. In his *Report on Faith* he gives a number of anecdotal reasons why episcopal conferences are not a good thing. Germany had an episcopal conference before the war, he points out, but the most vigorous anti-Nazi statements came not from this feeble body but from courageous individual bishops. To show that bishops just 'go with the crowd' he points out that at the second session of Vatican II in 1963 out of 2135 bishops only 200 managed to speak in St Peter's. 'The remaining ninety per cent never spoke and were restricted to listening and voting', declares Ratzinger, explaining that this is a feature of large groups which are 'democratic' only in appearance (*Rapporto sulla Fede*, pp. 59–60).

But evidently, these two anecdotes do not *prove* anything. If the German bishops had made a collective anti-Nazi statement it would obviously have made more impact. There was no *a priori* reason why they should have been incapable of that. It was not *because* they were an episcopal conference that they failed. The remark about the second session of Vatican II reveals an odd method of measuring participation: for the ninety per cent who did not speak in St Peter's probably were active in all kinds of other ways: submitting written amendments (more effective than speeches in the *aula*), studying the draft texts, taking part in the work of commissions, meeting bishops and theologians from other countries (practical collegiality), praying. They were not merely vote-fodder as Ratzinger seems to imagine. What an appalling judgement on the bishops of the Council is implied by these remarks. They seem no more than mindless sheep, waiting to be led.

Yet Ratzinger's ostensible aim is to rescue the bishop from the tyranny of the episcopal conference. He thinks it prevents the individual bishop from exercising his true responsibility. In his picture of an episcopal conference an active ginger-group impose their views on the silent majority of solid citizens. This can hardly be a reflection on his own brief experience as a member of the German episcopal conference between 1977 and 1981. They made no major decisions with which Ratzinger did not agree. Ratzinger got his way when, for example, they determined to go for a condemnation of Hans Küng. There is no example of him being bullied. So he must have other episcopal conferences in mind.

What Ratzinger now says of episcopal conferences smacks of rationalization. It may be that he is (no doubt unconsciously) using theological arguments to strengthen his own position of power in the Church. In other words, he is using theology ideologically, as a means of getting his own way. For it is evident that the Prefect of the CDF will find an individual bishop on his *ad limina* visit to Rome more pliable and docile than a self-confident episcopal conference on its own territory.

The Brazilian episcopal conference, for example, did not disguise its support for Leonardo Boff and sent two delegates to sit alongside him at his *colloquium* – thus destroying the Vatican myth that the liberation theologians have invented some 'popular Church' at odds with the hierarchy. The Brazilian bishops being too numerous to transform rapidly by new appointments (on the Dutch model), Ratzinger has to rely on the individual 'sound' bishops whom he can claim, somewhat implausibly, are 'really representative'. Thus he works through Cardinal Eugenio de Araújo Sales, Archbishop of Rio de Janeiro, his Swiss-born auxiliary, Karl Josef Romer, and Bonaventura Kloppenburg OFM. Kloppenburg once taught Leonardo Boff and has now become his principal foe.

The fact that John J. O'Connor rose so rapidly to the important see of New York and was quickly awarded a cardinal's hat (denied to other worthy and senior archbishops) suggests that the same policy may be applied to the United States. For O'Connor, a former military chaplain, a hawk, a lifelong Republican, has broken the 'seamless garment' policy of the US bishops. Cardinal Joseph Bernadin, Archbishop of Chicago, held that they should be consistently pro-life and oppose nuclear weapons with as much energy as they opposed abortion.

The truth of the matter is that an episcopal conference can stand up to Ratzinger. That is why he tries to cut them down to size. I have already said that it was unwise of him to enter the theological lists because, no longer able to rely on the authority of his office, his opinions would be no better than the arguments on which they were based. Thus by giving this extended interview, he exposed the fragility of his own position. It was very weak indeed. For although the term 'episcopal conference' was not used much until the 1917 code of canon law, they are in effect sort of 'standing committees', which bridge the gap between provincial councils (which used to be obligatory every twenty years). This point was made by the veteran canonist, Mgr Daniel Shanahan, who crushingly added: 'The provincial council is a very ancient body, much more ancient than the Roman Congregations and the office of Cardinal, and of more theological status than either' (letter to *The Tablet*, 22–29 December 1984, p. 1312).

Moreover, Ratzinger's attack on episcopal conferences would have the inevitable effect of uniting them in indignation against him. The reports to the Synod Secretariat would focus on the third of the four questions: 'Has the Council's doctrine on the universal Church and the particular church been rightly understood? Have internal relationships been established in the Church in a spirit of genuine collegiality and communion?'

That was the question that episcopal conferences all over the world were pondering in June and July. Ratzinger's interview set the agenda for the Extraordinary Synod – but not quite in the way he or the Pope may have intended.

6

Anglo-Saxon Attitudes

June and July 1985 were busy months for bishops. From Westminster, London, to Sydney, Australia, Collegeville, Minnesota, and all points of the compass, they brooded over what their response to the Synod Secretariat's question should be. To a man they lamented that the lack of time made serious consultation almost impossible. The President of the US Bishops' Conference, Bishop James Malone of Youngstown, Ohio, 'consulted' by means of an ingenious television phone-in programme. The English and Welsh bishops chose the more staid path of hearing diocesan and Catholic organizations including tiny right-wing ones like Fr Michael Clifton's *Vox: Vox* could not complain that it was silenced.

To tell the truth, and despite my previous chapter, there was very little talk about Ratzinger. When I asked Bishop Cormac Murphy O'Connor, of Arundel and Brighton, the Catholic Co-president of the Anglican Roman Catholic International Commission-II, whether the response of the English and Welsh bishops to ARCIC-I had been designed as a reply to Ratzinger's document on the same subject, he replied, gently but firmly, that the views of episcopal conferences had been sought and were rather more important than those of mere Roman Congregations. The same was true of responses to the Synod. But despite this bravado, there was disquieting news from Italy. One always has to attend to Italy to understand what is really happening in the Church. Enough bishops have studied in the Roman colleges and enough people were on the move in the summer months for Italian gossip to spread swiftly.

What had happened was most disconcerting. Cardinal Anastasio Ballestrero, Archbishop of Turin and a Carmelite, had just come to the end of his stint as President of the Italian Bishops' Conference (CEI). According to the CEI constitution, there was an election. Top of the poll was the Patriarch of Venice, Cardinal Marco Cé, second came Cardinal Carlo Maria Martini of Milan, and in last

63

and seventh place with only one vote (that of Cardinal Giuseppe Siri of Genoa) was the man known to be the papal candidate, Giacomo Biffi. The point at issue was the attitude to be adopted towards the lay movement *Communione e Liberazione*, founded in 1956.

CEI has made no secret of its detestation of *Communione e Liberazione* which is a spiritual cousin of Opus Dei. It represents a break with the 'spiritual option' of John XXIII and Paul VI. It is too redolent of the political Catholic Action of the 1950s when parish churches were recruiting stations for the Christian Democrats. Moreover, the 'secular arm' of *Communione Liberazione* forms a faction within the Christian Democrats called *Movimento Popolare*. Its leader got himself elected to the European Parliament in 1984. Pope John Paul cannot understand why the Italian bishops do not like it. He set aside their election and made the Cardinal Vicar of Rome, Ugo Poletti, President of the Italian Bishops' Conference. So the aged, sick, unelected Poletti would have to represent Italy at the Extraordinary Synod. Italy was disenfranchised. Poletti would not rock the boat. What his appointment really meant was that the Italian Bishops' Conference, having the misfortune to be on the papal doorstep, was being treated as though it were merely a dicastery (or department) of the Roman Curia.

It is not always easy even for bishops to know what is happening in the Church. Archbishop Francis Roberts Rush of Brisbane, who would represent Australia at the Synod, came away from the meeting of the bishops of Oceania in June with a new spring in his step: 'Wonderful things have taken place as a result of the Council. We can only be positive about the coming Synod'.

A discerning fly on the wall at the US bishops' meeting in Collegeville would have heard a different story. The US bishops are a remarkably cohesive lot. They are not Ratzingerian sheep. As they saw it, the key question was whether the Church is meant to be a 'top-down' or a 'bottom-up' organization. Is each diocese fully Church and are all dioceses together the expression of the universal Church? Recent Roman interventions (out of respect no one said interference) in US dioceses made these questions very topical. There was grave concern about the way the Curia claimed the right to investigate the orthodoxy of local bishops and their seminaries.

As for the Extraordinary Synod, attitudes among the US bishops at Collegeville ranged from 'quiet alarm' to a near total dismissal of the event as trivial. Too many ceremonial happenings were foreseen and, anyway, there would not be time to tackle any topic in depth. Some held that the Extraordinary Synod would be little more than a platform permitting Pope John Paul to place his stamp of disapproval on a wide range of Vatican II concerns. The more optimistic said that any attempt to repeal Vatican II would be vain, since one could not undo in two weeks what had taken four years to accomplish.

But perhaps the dominant impression in Collegeville was that despite Ratzinger's statements on the nullity of episcopal conferences, the US bishops intended to forge ahead with their pastoral letter on economic morality. The Extraordinary Synod was regarded at best as an opportunity for 'honest evaluation'. But mostly they thought it was their duty to make the best of a bad job.

Bishop Malone's address to them was consciously presented as only an 'interim estimate' of Vatican II. He was very positive:

> Not only am I convinced that Pope John and the Council were correct concerning the proper role for the Church in our times, I am also convinced that we have been fundamentally on the right track in seeking to bring it about. (*Origins*, 4 July 1985)

This assurance was important: Malone was optimistic not just about the Council itself but about the way it had been implemented. Thus he struck a blow against the Council–OK, its interpretations not–OK attitude.

Again Malone rejected Cardinal Joseph Ratzinger's idea of 'restoration' by denouncing the fallacy of some pre-conciliar utopia. He shrewdly linked this with what Pope John XXIII had said on the opening day of the Council:

> The prophets of gloom of whom Pope John spoke are still very much with us. They would have it that the last two decades have witnessed nothing but dissolution and collapse, and that the Church can only be saved by returning to some earlier, fictitious golden age. While sympathizing with their undoubtedly sincere prescriptions, I do not believe that we can accept either their analysis or their prescriptions. (*Origins*, ibid., p. 100)

Cardinal Ratzinger (never of course mentioned) was even more firmly shown the exit in the following passage which not only declares that the US bishops really *do* possess a mandate to teach, which they intend to go on using, but asserts that they know of no better way to teach:

> I hope to be able to share with the Synod my profound conviction that our experience in the United States has been on the whole

a very positive one. I do not share the view that episcopal conferences ought not to play too large or active a role in the life of the
Church. Consider the tremendous contribution our conference
has made to the public debate on war and peace or our current
grappling with Catholic social teaching and the US economy.
How could we have made these and other positive contributions
except through our episcopal conference? I look forward to
sharing these thoughts and more at the Synod. (*Origins,* ibid.,
p. 101)

Yet Malone's jaunty, can-do approach did not blind him to the
ambivalence of the Council and the negative effects which sometimes followed it.

So 'optimism' had to be balanced by a realistic appraisal of
failure:

We also need to take seriously the evidence that many of our
people in these years have grown less firm in their belief, less
apostolic in their practice, more self-absorbed and inward-looking
in their attitude to things both spiritual and secular.

Yet this is obviously not the whole story.

Side by side with those of whom this is true, we find countless
examples of persons who have interiorized the authentic spirit of
Vatican II and grasped that the Christian vocation to the world
is not a pious platitude but a necessary consequence of incorpor-
ation into Christ through baptism. (*Origins*, ibid., p. 101)

Though Malone joked that he could not speak for all the US bishops
– nearly three hundred of them – he had in fact caught the mood
of the meeting and their eventual report, published on 16 September
1985, reflected exactly what he had said at Collegeville in June.

However, the report of the US bishops did add one crucially
important thought. Whatever one might think of the negative factors
in US Catholicism today, the Council itself was not to be blamed
for them. Rather 'cultural factors originating outside the Catholic
Church account for many recent problems of Catholic life in the
United States as in many other countries'. So allegedly unorthodox
theologians were not to be made the scapegoats. Malone made quite
clear in June and September what position the US bishops would
adopt: they were unrepentant on collegiality. Ratzinger might
dismiss their position as 'pragmatic' rather than 'theological'. But
they were used to that and not worried (or fazed) by it. The late
Fr Gustave Weigel sj used to distinguish between the 'continental

mind' and the 'Anglo-Saxon mind'. His German accent thickened as he explained that for the 'continental mind' you do not have an agreement unless it is written down and spelled out in the fullest juridical detail; while the 'Anglo-Saxon mind' believes that on the whole the less law the better, and that much can be left to common sense (see Xavier Rynne, *The Second Session*, 1964, p. 198).

The English and Welsh bishops would rather like to be described as 'pragmatic'. Their report was unexpectedly made public on 29 July. Vatican diplomats later said that publication of the reports went 'against the norms'. But that was not likely to deter Cardinal Basil Hume and his colleagues. They wanted to strike fast and get in first. Their document showed that they were capable of theological reflection of a high order, and that they had to hand the best theologians not just in Britain but in Europe. Their 'submission' was not in the least submissive.

What made it important was that it was from start to finish a vote of confidence in the Council's continuing vitality and an outright, even brutal, rejection of the pessimism in vogue in the Roman Curia. What made it historic was that our bishops had never before publicly admitted that there could be any hint of a quarrel with the Curia. Clerical gossip picked up the tail-end of the inevitable rows, of course, but officially they did not happen. As Cardinal John Carmel Heenan assured his cronies, a private word in the ear of the Prefect of the Holy Office was much more effective than public remonstrances that 'only helped the Church's enemies'. But now, even as they submitted the out-spoken document to Rome, the bishops actually published it. They had been *asked* for their opinion. They gave it freely.

Cardinal Ratzinger, having done most of the talking over the previous twelve months, was now obliged to listen. He had already been tackled by various theologians. But now he had a new and more formidable opponent: a solidly united episcopal conference that did not propose to yield to any theological intimidation or curial bullying. The 'submission' also showed that the English and Welsh bishops had found a way of working effectively together. They thanked the US bishops who had shown them how to do it: 'The way in which the US bishops' pastoral letter on peace was composed holds lessons of wider importance about the exercise of authority with dialogue'. This answered Ratzinger's point that the US bishops had 'no mandate' to teach. And Ratzinger's insistence that bishops should only teach when they can bind in conscience was dismissed with the remark that there were other teaching styles, notably 'a form of teaching that fosters dialogue'.

Then they counterattack by observing, without naming any names, that 'many formal teaching documents are too long and complex to be effective'. Did that include the Pope's speeches? No one would go quite that far, but one prelate privately remarked that an average of three papal speeches a day put the credibility of the ordinary *magisterium* under severe strain. The *magisterium* would be all the more effective for being used sparingly, relevantly and economically. One should not, in short, devalue the currency of the *magisterium*.

But the defence of the theological status and reality of episcopal conferences was not just based on the fact that they worked. The English and Welsh bishops quote a little-noticed passage in *Lumen Gentium* which compares episcopal conferences to the ancient patri-archal sees. The diversity 'of liturgical usage and theological and spiritual patrimony' of local churches, 'notably the ancient patriar-chal churches', is seen as showing 'all the more resplendently the catholicity of the undivided Church'. *Lumen Gentium* then concludes: 'In like fashion the episcopal conferences at the present time are in a position to contribute in many fruitful ways to the concrete realiz-ation of the collegiate spirit' (23). No new patriarchates can be created (Venice and Lisbon are the only examples in the last millen-nium and they have an artificial air), but the episcopal conference has the task they habitually had: handing on the faith in their own cultural milieu and in a language that makes sense to the local people.

The episcopal 'submission' illustrates this point by its very frank-ness. Roman Catholics in Britain are in a minority. So they cannot impose their views on a pluralistic society: they have to argue for them. The bishops seem to think this is on the whole a bracingly healthy situation. It is very different from, say, Poland or perhaps Spain. It has made for what they call 'greater sensitivity in pastoral care to the difficulties of specific situations', with a reference to Pope John Paul's remarks at Knavesmire racecourse, York, where he had spoken more hopefully about mixed marriages than else-where: 'You live in your marriages the hopes and difficulties of the path to Christian unity'. The joke was that they had drafted the speech for him. But the case for 'pluralism' is not merely a sturdy defence of the rights of episcopal conferences against centralization and uniformity. It is ultimately based on the very nature of a bishop, on what a bishop is for.

People are accustomed to seeing the bishop as the focus of unity in the diocese, and so he is. But he is also the guardian and promoter of diversity in the Church. This was how *Lumen Gentium* defined the mission of the Bishop of Rome, the successor or Vicar of St Peter: 'The Chair of Peter presides over the whole assembly of charity and protects their legitimate variety while at the same time taking care that these differences do not hinder unity, but rather contribute to it' (23). Striking the right balance is admittedly not very easy in such matters, but the English and Welsh bishops prefer to err on the side of tolerance. They say:

> Greater emphasis should be placed in catechesis and teaching on true unity rather than on uniformity of practice. The ecumenical movement is both a help and a beneficiary in this matter. Consideration should now be given to developing a common catechesis based on what has already been ecumenically accepted.

One hardly dares say it, but what Catholics call 'pluralism', Anglicans call 'comprehensiveness'.

Other features of the British cultural scene that have changed the Church for the better are the influx of immigrants from the Commonwealth, the development of prayer groups and of theological studies among the laity, and, biting most deeply of all, the ecumenical movement of which they say: 'The achievements of the ecumenical movement have demonstrated the richness and potential complementarity of diverse Christian traditions'. All these elements are thrown into the pluralistic pot. They stimulate more than they alarm. And the plea for diversity, stated along these lines for England and Wales, applies self-evidently also to Brazil and liberation theology.

All of which reverses so many conventional habits of thought that it is worth pausing for a moment to grasp its implications. Much Catholic apologetic from the Counter-Reformation onwards was based on the contrast between the Roman Catholic Church which 'knew where it stood' and was the rock of unity against which the waves of error lashed in vain, and 'Protestants' who relied on 'scripture alone' and so split into innumerable sects. It was an apologetic based on immutability. But taught by John Henry Newman and Vatican II the English and Welsh bishops recognize the place of development in Catholic doctrine and the crucial importance of responding to what the Holy Spirit is saying now (the 'signs of the times'). This results in a different 'apologetic' or, as the bishops call it, process of 'evangelization' in which the vitality of the Church is its drawing-power, not the fact that it has all the answers. So they explain:

> Effective evangelization needs to recognize the hand of God in the world. Questions which preoccupy the hearts and minds of people today must contribute significantly to preaching, teaching, formation and ongoing spiritual renewal in the Church.

So to those who explain the 'crisis' in the Church by the vagaries of theologians and seek to protect the 'simple faithful' from their supposed depredations, the English and Welsh bishops coolly offer an alternative explanation:

> Because of the previous relative simplicity of expression of the Church's teaching, present diversities in expression and also in pastoral practice have disturbed some of the faithful.

So the explanation for the 'crisis' is that it was the result of new knowledge meeting old prejudice. This was confirmed by the remark that 'a lack of tolerance and a certain new fundamentalism have led to strong expressions of extreme minority opinion'. This referred equally to the heresy-hunting little magazines of the right and the 'Down-with-Rome' cries on the left.

The crucial difference between the analysis offered by the English and Welsh bishops and that of Ratzinger is that while he lays the blame on those who advocate changes, they blame rather those who resist change. They say:

> Implementing the decrees of Vatican II has placed a heavy responsibility on priests and bishops. Where they have been open to change, this has enabled renewal to take place; where they have not been open to change, this has hindered the process of renewal.

They give the example of ecumenism, but the same principle would apply to liturgy, spiritual direction, social commitment and much else besides. Moreover, they seem to be inviting the laity to take initiatives when they remark:

> While many more lay people are now aware of their baptismal calling, traditionally the laity have been over-dependent on the leadership of the clergy.

Where Rome might see an incitement to mutiny, the English and Welsh bishops see a release of charismatic and ministerial energy. What they say about women reflects this. First a confession:

70

'There has been a failure to come to terms with the role of women in the Church'. Then a 'suggestion':

> There must be a concerted effort by the whole Church to be open to the changing role of women, which has many implications for the life of the Church. In addition, attention must be paid to the problem of exclusive language, especially in the liturgy. These questions are causing some disquiet and will undoubtedly grow in importance during the next decade.

This is not so vague or jejune as it may sound. In 1980 the US bishops recommended that the eucharistic prayers should be revised 'to eliminate the exclusively male tone of the original language'. This was rejected by the Congregation for Divine Worship on the grounds that 'the problem is universal – the whole English-speaking world must move together or not at all'. Explaining this refusal, Fr Cuthbert Johnson OSB said that he 'objected to individual groups or movements claiming to the right to change the meaning of words, such as mankind or man' (*National Catholic Reporter*, 16 November 1984). The English and Welsh bishops are more prepared to accept that 'usage' determines meaning, and that how women feel about 'male' language matters: the disquiet will not go away by being mocked or ignored.

After such a daring claim, the suggestion that women should be admitted to the ministries of Reader and Acolyte may seem an anticlimax. But it is a good place to start. What were once regarded as 'minor orders', steps on the road to the priesthood, are now described as 'ministries'. The future ordained minister must pass through these stages, the male may come to rest in them, but the female may not. This ban makes little sense but has great symbolic importance.

Penultimately, there are some more 'professional' complaints which one probably needs to be a bishop fully to appreciate. 'Collegiality' is not working properly, they say (under 'difficulties and failures'), because 'there are signs of a lessening of the involvement and real responsibility of members of bishops' conferences in the membership and consultancy of the organisms of the Holy See'. The reforms of Pope Paul VI in 1967 admitted diocesan bishops as consultors to all Roman Congregations. The grumble is that regular meetings are no longer held, that the annual plenary meeting is often rigged, and that the diocesan bishops, instead of being regarded as valuable witnesses to the experience of their local churches, are now reduced to being no more than part of the conveyor-belt of the system. They particularly resent the way the law on dispensations from priestly obligations was arbitrarily changed, leaving them with intractable pastoral and human problems.

Finally, the English and Welsh bishops reflect on the Synod itself, considered as an institution: 'The Synod of bishops should be seen as a more effective expression of collegiality, and its processes revised in the light of experience'. They meant that the experience of previous Synods had been rather discouraging.

More immediately, they expressed their 'concern' about 'the preparation, course and aftermath' of the Extraordinary Synod to which all these remarks were meant to be a contribution. 'Concern' is the ecclesiastical word for alarm and gloom. Optimistic so far, the English and Welsh bishops were apprehensive about the impending event. They spelled out the reasons:

1. The time for preparation, consultation and submission of experience of particular churches is short. This means that the analysis of the effects of the Council is necessarily limited.

2. The process of the Synod itself, the drawing up of the agenda and preparatory papers, the allocation of time to the diverse elements of ceremonial celebrations, set addresses, discussions in smaller groups and general debate all need to be arranged very carefully. The process should be geared towards allowing the mind of the Synod to be fully articulated for the benefit of the whole Church.

There was a contrast here between the putative 'mind of the Synod' which they hope would be expressed, and the pre-planning which, it was intimated, might prevent this.

Perhaps this was why Cardinal Basil Hume at his press conference advised that one should 'keep the Synod in perspective'. One should not expect too much of it. It would be sufficient if disaster were averted. The really decisive moment would come not at the Extraordinary Synod but at the Synod on 'the Vocation and Mission of the Laity in the Church and the World' in autumn 1987. Thus the problem was to 'negotiate' the 1985 Synod without too many mishaps. The last word of the bishops is:

The Church of England and Wales looks to the Extraordinary Synod for a clear and positive reaffirmation of the spirit and decrees of Vatican II, and wishes to hear a word of encouragement for all who have worked so hard for renewal in the life of the Church.

It remained to ask what had emboldened the English and Welsh bishops to speak out so vigorously and what the effects of their statement were likely to be. One very simple fact may have helped. The Vatican is not lily-white in financial matters and is therefore less able to lecture the world on public morality. The bishops note this delicately (rather curiously under the heading 'difficulties and failures in the ministries of the Church'): 'It is felt that a clear presentation of the affairs of the patrimony of the Holy See is lacking'. Translate: what answer are you going to give to David Yallop's *In God's Name*, which has caused immense harm, embarrassment and scandal? Lordly disdain does not seem an adequate reply.

On a deeper level, one can say that the ARCIC experience has had a greater effect than anyone realized. Thus the use of *koinonia* or communion as the model in thinking about the Church is not just to be wheeled out on special ecumenical occasions. On the contrary it enters deeply into the Church's self-understanding at all levels and has practical consequences. One of them is that the relationship between the Bishop of Rome as 'universal primate' and the bishops of the Church is not one of king to subjects. Bishops are not like branch managers in the RC Multinational Company Inc. The essence of unity consists in 'being in communion with' not in 'taking orders from'. This is not to deny that the Bishop of Rome has the indispensable function of making unity visible and, in certain limited and extreme circumstances, of settling doctrinal disputes. The English and Welsh bishops quote an interesting contribution to the Vatican I debates on infallibility. The purpose of the definition was to preserve the truth in the Church (*conservatio veritatis in ecclesia*) and it was to 'operate when individual bishops or provincial councils were unable to deal with divisions in matters of faith satisfactorily in their own right' (with reference to Mansi's *Acts of Vatican I*, vol. 52, no. 1213). But that does not describe the present situation. Thus the doctrine of *koinonia* combines with the principle of subsidiarity (never put up to a higher level what can be dealt with on a lower level) to enable the English and Welsh bishops to speak out with such confidence.

The decision to publish this 'submission' meant that the English and Welsh bishops had seized the initiative on the international scene. They had set out an agenda for the Synod that would make sense of it. They had acted on public opinion in the Church and created expectations about the Extraordinary Synod. They could expect a lot of support from other episcopal conferences. Since

Cardinal Basil Hume was President of the Council of European Bishops, he already knew the mind of the Europeans. The English and Welsh bishops could assume this 'leading role' all the more easily because of their blameless past and record of docility. No one had ever suspected them of Dutch excesses. No British theologian had been condemned since the Modernist period. Vatican II had been assimilated with painful slowness. But this now turned out to be an advantage. These were clearly not 'dissident' bishops or cantankerous 'rebels' but practical pastoral chaps who knew when to consult theologians (the reference to Mansi in the previous paragraph was not at every bishop's fingertips). So the English and Welsh bishops knew what they were doing. They may have done more than they knew.

One should not underestimate the personal role of Cardinal Basil Hume in all this. In an interview with Kevin O'Kelly, of Irish Radio, Hume explained that the emphasis on 'pluralism' in the document was 'not a defence of self-interest, but a service to the Church'. 'We have enough immigrants in the country', he explained, 'to know about pluralism, whether secular or ecclesial.' This sense of pluralism comes easily to a Benedictine abbot, for the Benedictines are natural 'federalists' and never had an abbot-general until the Vatican imposed one on them in the late nineteenth century. Again as a monk, Fr Basil is used to giving and receiving 'fraternal correction' which is not only permissible in the Church but, for a cardinal, a duty. As a bishop who was an abbot, he tries to govern according to chapter 64 of the Rule of St Benedict. It says that 'the monastery should be so organized that the strong have something to strive for, while the weak are not weighed down by burdens too crushing to bear' (see Basil Hume, *Searching for God*, 1977, p. 13). He also knows the international scene well. And he knows the value of 'lived parables'. While Ratzinger was busy condemning Leonardo Boff, Hume was in famine-stricken Ethiopia.

But the strength of the 'submission' from the English and Welsh bishops is precisely that it is not just the elucubrations of an individual. The bishops have been thinking about Vatican II for a long time. It has shaped their pastoral policies. The faithful have been consulted first in the National Pastoral Congress held in Liverpool in May 1980: the surprise was that 'ordinary' Catholics as well as Thames Valley intellectuals were discovered to share a set of attitudes which all assumed that Vatican II was the most encouraging and grace-filled event that had happened in their lifetime. The 1985 consultation was briefer, but since it covered the same ground, it did not need to be so extensive. Recent episcopal appointments have also strengthened Cardinal Hume's position. And the return of Bishop Agnellus Andrew from Rome, where he was Pro-president of the Pontifical Commission for the Means of Social Communication, meant that the bishops now have in their midst a shrewd connoisseur of the Vatican who can tell them how far they can go. At the Synod Cardinal Hume could speak in the name of the Church in England and Wales. So from every point of view, Cardinal Hume was in a very strong position.

But a wise leader also looks to the future. It was not enough to save the 1985 Synod from disaster and to prepare the ground for the doctrinally much more important 1987 one. This explains the most curious remark in the document. Among the 'suggestions' on 'collegiality' we find: 'Due attention should be given to the voice of the local bishops in the appointment of bishops'. They can hardly be saying that this principle has not been observed so far, for then they would be complaining about their own appointments. Archbishop Bruno Heim, the Pro-Nuncio, had had a hand in the appointment of a record forty of them. But Heim went home to Switzerland in July 1985 almost at the same time as this episcopal submission was sent to Rome. So this remark warns in effect that the Holy See would be ill-advised to try 'the Dutch solution': briefing the new Pro-Nuncio to recommend ultra-conservative bishops out of sympathy with their clergy and people.

Ampleforth is a rugby school and Basil Hume was a keen rugby coach. With this document he broke through the middle of the field and raced for the line, the rest of the pack following at his heels. He would prove difficult to bring down, except by a trip or an unaccountable blast on the referee's whistle or a change in the rules of the game.

7

Dress Rehearsals

In August Archbishop Jan Schotte, who had succeeded Cardinal Tomko as Secretary of the Synod Secretariat, cut short his holidays and began 'processing' the first replies from episcopal conferences. In September he was joined by Walter Kasper, the Tübingen theologian, who was appointed Secretary for the Extraordinary Synod. The names of the papal nominees were announced in October. There were some surprising omissions: neither Joseph Bernadin, Chicago, nor Carlo Maria Martini, Milan, nor Evaristo Arns, São Paulo, Brazil, were included. The veteran Cardinals Léon-Joseph Suenens, Malines-Brussels, and Franz König, Vienna, who could have witnessed to the aims of Vatican II of which they were among the principal architects, were likewise omitted. (König was brought in later, as an afterthought.) This seemed to stack the Synod in one direction. On the other hand the nomination of the three presidents looked like an attempt to balance conflicting tendencies in the Church: Cardinal John J. Krol of Philadelphia represented the good old days, Cardinal Joseph Malula of Kinshasha, Zaire, stood for 'Africanization' (he had proposed a 'Council' for Africa in 1980), while Cardinal Jan Willebrands kept the tattered ecumenical flag flying.

But it was possible that these nominations were largely honorific. The task of presidents is to sit there looking grand and sagacious. Much more important was the appointment of Suenens' successor in Malines-Brussels, Cardinal Godfried Danneels, as *Relator* or *rapporteur* of the Synod. The shorter the Synod, the more important it was to get the questions right from the outset. This would be the task of Danneels. Thus by October all the main participants in the Synod had been assigned their roles. This chapter will examine what they were doing and saying in the run-up to the Synod. The main protagonists were Pope John Paul himself, Walter Kasper, Godfried Danneels, and – since this was after all a Synod of *bishops*

– Basil Hume who continued, under increasingly testing circumstances, to try to influence the outcome.

Pope John Paul did not have much of a holiday in August.
Instead the indefatigable pontiff went on a marathon journey to
Africa which ended with an unforgettable and unprecedented
meeting with sixty thousand young Moslems in a stadium in Casa-
blanca, Morocco. But the most important contribution to the theme
of the Extraordinary Synod came in Nairobi, Kenya, on Sunday 19
August 1985. It had been a busy day: John Paul had concluded the
43rd Eucharistic Congress, planted a ceremonial tree in Uhuru Park
(it was an olea), and addressed the United Nations Environment
Department. He then solemnly inaugurated the Catholic Higher
Institute of East Africa (CHIEA) which would, he said, 'have a
role to play in implementing for East Africa the *dynamism* of the
second Vatican Council'. He seemed, therefore, to be espousing the
view of the English and Welsh bishops in their 'submission': the
full implications of the Council have not yet been felt in the Catholic
world.

But this apparently clear endorsement of the Council was hedged
about with so many qualifications that it came closer to the pessimism of Cardinal Joseph Ratzinger than to the optimism of the US
and English and Welsh bishops. There was a basic misunderstanding about the reasons why Pope John XXIII had summoned
the Council, and therefore about what the Synod would commemorate. Everything said in chapter 2 now came home with full force.
Yet Pope John Paul appealed in Nairobi to the authority of his
predecessor:

> Let us never forget those words spoken by Pope John XXIII on
> the opening day of the collegial assembly: 'The greatest concern
> of the Ecumenical Council is this: that the sacred deposit of faith
> should be more effectively guarded and taught'.

This sentence does indeed occur in the magnificent opening address
to the Council into which the eighty-year-old Pope poured all the
wisdom and experience of his long life. But it does not convey the
whole of what he wanted the Council to do. Its main point or
thrust, what Pope John called the *punctum saliens*, was not merely
defensive, as he carefully explained:

> The salient point of this Council is not, therefore, a discussion of
> one or other article of the fundamental doctrines of the Church
> which have been repeatedly taught by the Fathers and by ancient

and modern theologians and which may be presumed to be well known and familiar to all. *For this a Council was not necessary.* (Abbott, p. 715)

So for Pope John the point of the Council was not merely to repeat what was already known. It was to bring about what he called a 'leap forward' in the understanding of the Gospel, to clothe traditional faith in a new language for, as he explained, 'the substance of the ancient doctrine of faith is one thing, the way it is presented is another' (ibid.).

This was the most important single sentence Pope John ever uttered. It set the agenda for bishops and theologians and the whole Church for the next twenty years. It opened the Church up to the dimension of time. It was the reason why Pope John could say that his Council was not called to denounce errors. 'Today', he said on that memorable 11 October 1962, 'the Spouse of Christ prefers to make use of the medicine of mercy rather than that of severity.' The most thorough study of the genesis of Pope John's inaugural speech confirms that his intention was that the Council was to be pastoral and positive rather than negative and defensive (see Giuseppe Alberigo and Alberto Melloni, 'L'allocuzione *Gaudet Mater Ecclesia* di Giovanni XXIII', in *Fede Tradizione Profezia*, 1984). Or as the US delegate to the Synod, Bishop James Malone, put it: 'Pope John's charge to Vatican II was a twofold mandate: unswerving fidelity and bold creativity' (*Origins*, 4 July 1985, p. 100).

But once Pope John Paul had redefined the purpose of the Council in this way, he had an easy transition to grim warnings about 'dangerous theologians':

> The dangers of a theological study which is divorced from life in the Spirit, and the harm caused by a pseudo-theological culture devoid of a genuine spirit of service to the mystery of redemption are, in a sense, evoked by the solemn words of St John: 'Every spirit which does not confess Jesus is not of God. This is the spirit of anti-Christ' (1 John 4:3).

Had some theologians fallen into this trap? More relevantly in the context of Nairobi, had some *African* theologians been thus ensnared by anti-Christ? If Pope John Paul did not believe this, then his lurid and melodramatic language was disproportionate. But since no one in particular was named, it could not be libellous, and African theologians could either say that these remarks did not really concern them or quake in their boots wondering who was next for the dungeons.

John Paul, however, conceded that theology had to deal with the new problems thrown up by life in the twentieth century. That provides the raw material for theology. But he suggested that the answers to these new problems were already contained in the *magisterium*:

> In order to be truly Christian, this theological reflection must be guided by the revealed word of God and the teaching of the Church as it has developed from the beginning through the exercise of the prophetic office of Christ, which has been *transmitted in a particular way to the Roman Pontiff and to the bishops who are in communion with him* (italics in the text).

Now it would be extremely difficult to prove, historically, that this concept of Pope and bishops possessing an exclusive monopoly of the Spirit has been held 'from the beginning'. In the thirteenth century the word *magisterium* meant the body of the *magistri*, those who taught theology in the universities of Oxford, Paris and Bologna. They were represented in their own right at Councils right up to Trent in the sixteenth century. *Magisterium* only shifted from theologians to bishops in a late and long process of development that culminated in Vatican I.

So it was the teaching of Vatican I rather than Vatican II that shaped John Paul's remarks in Nairobi about 'freedom of research':

> While a rightful and necessary freedom of research is essential in the progress of theological science, those engaged in theological investigations should not understand this freedom as the transposition into the field of theology of methodological criteria borrowed from other sciences. Christian theology has its specific point of departure in the Word of God transmitted in the scriptures, and it possesses a constant point of reference in the Church's *magisterium, the authentic guardian and interpreter of the full doctrine of Christ* (italics in the text).

Apart from the historical point, was this the most important message for African theologians in 1985? They have to contend with poverty, shanty-towns, malnutrition, famine, up-rooted peasants, one-party states, friendly or unfriendly military regimes, *apartheid* in South Africa, the collapse of the traditional culture of the tribe (in which everyone had a place), and the Moslem threat reaching almost half-way down the continent.

So there was some disappointment among African theologians at the abstract tenor of this address. Because they inherited without having caused the conflicts which split the Church in Europe in the sixteenth century, they are keen ecumenists and have assimilated *Dei Verbum*, the Council's document on divine revelation (together with *Lumen Gentium*, the only Council text described as a 'dogmatic constitution'). They know that *Dei Verbum* subordinates the *magisterium* itself to scripture and tradition, and that this is a condition of the ecumenical enterprise. Yet the Pope's words in Nairobi seemed to reverse this relationship by making the *magisterium* 'a constant point of reference'. At least John Paul did not say '*the* constant point of reference'.

But the message to the Synod from Nairobi was clear enough. Though Pope John Paul half disavowed Cardinal Joseph Ratzinger in the plane on the way back, he agreed with him on the most crucial question: jumped-up theologians had misinterpreted the Council and were filled with the spirit of anti-Christ.

This is not a description anyone could apply to Walter Kasper, who was one of the youngest professors to be appointed in Germany. Now fifty-two, he was a mere stripling in ecclesiastical terms when he was appointed Secretary of the Extraordinary Synod. Obviously he would do his secretarial work with computer-like objectivity and not try to hijack the Synod. Yet his personal views on the present state of the Church were not without interest if one wanted to predict the way the Synod would go. Kasper is a fortunate man in one respect: he does not enter the field of theology with any labels round his neck. Indeed, to define his unique contribution to theology, I cannot do better than transcribe what Fr Aidan Nichols OP had to say about him:

> Walter Kasper is the leading living representative of the Tübingen school. Author of a critical evaluation of the fundamental theology of the Roman school in the nineteenth century (where Cardinal Perrone crossed swords with Newman over the latter's subtle and delicate portrait of doctrinal development), Kasper stands self-consciously in the long line of Möhler, Geiselmann and Karl Adam, and therefore at the antipodes of anything that might resemble a 'court theology' of the papal households. ('The Pope and his critics', *The Tablet*, 9 March 1985, p. 244)

This judgement was particularly valuable in that it was made in ignorance of Kasper's appointment as Secretary of the Synod.

But what did Walter Kasper really think about Vatican II? There was no need to grope for an answer, for Kasper had written a paper on this very topic to guide the German bishops in their deliberations. True, it had not been released to the press. But since it was a credit to its author, it was difficult to think of any serious reason for keeping it secret.

Kasper revealed himself as a 'moderate' but in the best sense of the term: he had measured the extremes and found them wanting. He rejected the neurotic pessimism of his former colleague, Joseph Ratzinger, as firmly as he rejected the 'We-were-robbed-of-the-Council' judgement of Hans Küng, who was still a Tübingen colleague of his – though deprived of his licence to teach as a Catholic theologian. It would be possible to present the entire Synod scenario as a discussion between three West German professors in a Tübingen seminar-room. But that would no doubt be an over-simplification.

Kasper is refreshingly blunt. His approach to the Council was wholly positive. He said: 'The Council is and was a sign and witness of the Holy Spirit in the Church. It has thrown fresh light in an attractive way on the idea and form of Catholicism today'. Of course, he went on, one had to see the Council as a whole. There must be no picking or choosing among its texts. In particular: 'One should give neither a legalistic and over-literal interpretation of the Council, forgetting its spirit . . . nor try to play off the spirit of the Council against its actual texts'.

Kasper agreed with Ratzinger (and almost everybody else) in repudiating the idea that the Council meant that the Church had gone back to square one and started from scratch: 'One cannot make a distinction between pre-conciliar and post-conciliar as though the post-conciliar Church were a "new Church", and as though the true Church only then emerged from an immensely long dark age to rediscover the original meaning of the Gospel'. It remained unclear who these theologians were who said that Vatican II represented a totally new departure. Just for the record, I would like to quote a passage from a book I wrote ten years ago:

Of course the distinction between pre-conciliar and post-conciliar should not be pushed to the length of absurdity – though in the excitement it frequently was, the Council was transformed into one of those pills which appear to work a miraculous change between 'before' and 'after'. There was an underlying continuity between pre-conciliar and post-conciliar, and if one tries hard enough one can see how the seeds of almost every conciliar doctrine were sown in the years which preceded it. (Peter Hebble-thwaite, *The Runaway Church*, 1975, pp. 10–11)

But that does not entail the idea that the Council had nothing fresh to say or was mere repetition, old hat. One can have creativity within fidelity, novelty within tradition, as Kasper admits.

But what about the 'crisis' in the Church? Kasper concedes that the Church has undergone many difficulties since Vatican II. But he denies that they were caused by the Council. The years 1965–85 in Western Europe and North America (Kasper, a careful scholar, pleads ignorance of the rest of the world) coincided with 'a kind of cultural revolution which led to a break with tradition, a crisis of authority, an indifference towards questions of faith, great uncertainty about moral values, and a crisis in the realm of ethics'. These pressures were felt within the Church, not surprisingly Kasper remarks, since the Church can never be hermetically sealed off from the 'world' (and those whose main aim is to remain uncontaminated by the world turn the Church into a 'sect').

Kasper at this early stage (April) thought that the four great constitutions of the Council (other documents were in the genre of decrees or declarations) would provide the ground-plan for the Synod. But he soon rallied to Cardinal Carlo Maria Martini's view that in practice it would have to be restricted to the dogmatic constitution on the Church (*Lumen Gentium*) and the pastoral consti-tution on the Church in the modern world (*Gaudium et Spes*).

Lumen Gentium has had more influence on the life of the Church, noted Kasper. It brought a new self-understanding of the Church. This seed has fallen on rich ground: 'The sense of co-responsibility has been strengthened, above all among lay people, and it has been put into practice in manifold forms of co-operation. The Church is once again understood and experienced as *communio*'. One positive effect is that 'the unity of the Church is perceived as a unity between local churches, and therefore understood and lived as diversity in unity'.

However, Kasper maintains that *Lumen Gentium* has been selec-tively read and 'received'. Ratzinger made the same remark. But while Ratzinger claimed that chapter 2 on the People of God had blotted out the memory of chapter 3 on the hierarchy, Kasper thought that both these chapters had been well received and that the sadly neglected passage was chapter 5 on the universal call to holiness. This remark could lead to questions about the canoniz-ation policy of the Congregation for the Causes of Saints, which continues to favour priests and religious men and women, leaving lay and married people with very few 'models' of holiness.

On the actual exercise of authority in the Church, Kasper thought that there is still a long way to go towards realizing the principles of *Lumen Gentium*: 'On all levels of Church life collegiality (understood in its broadest sense) and participation (dialogue, co-responsibility, involvement in decision-making) in the spirit of the Council are desirable, indeed necessary'. Kasper adds – exclamation mark his own: 'In this respect not all the legitimate(!) expectations of Vatican II have been fulfilled'.

This all sounds rather abstract and German professorial. Kasper had no need to give instances of the failure of collegiality and consultation. That was not his brief. His readers could supply their own examples. But at the Catholic Academy in Munich on 12 October he went out of his way to praise the Christian character and pastoral achievements of theologians like Leonardo Boff and – to applause – to distance himself from Cardinal Ratzinger's moves against him. This echoed the complaint of the Brazilian bishops that they had not been consulted before the Congregation for the Doctrine of Faith's Instruction 'On certain forms of liberation theology'. The Munich episode showed that Kasper was perfectly prepared publicly to disagree with Ratzinger. So unless Kasper lost his nerve, the fear that the Synod script would be prompted by Ratzinger was unlikely to prove true.

The implementation of *Gaudium et Spes*, Kasper admits, posed greater problems than *Lumen Gentium*. For the project was utterly novel: no Council had ever before tried to state the Church's relationship with the world. No doubt the description of the 'signs of the times' in the opening chapters of *Gaudium et Spes* was somewhat dated and bore traces of the 'optimism' of the mid 1960s. But *Gaudium et Spes* offered a method as well as a message; and it was the method that had to be applied anew in each generation. For Kasper the properly theological questions raised by *Gaudium et Spes* are: how is an eternal truth reflected in historical reality?, how is the identity of the Gospel proclamation to be maintained through the diversity of times, cultures and situations in which it is lived out? Slogans like 'signs of the times' and 'inculturation' have their uses, but they do not resolve the crucial question which concerns truth.

Kasper's conclusion struck a final blow at Ratzingerian pessimism: 'In my opinion it would be entirely wrong for the Synod simply to utter a great cry of lamentation about the problems and the evidence of crisis. The positive achievements must also be recognized'. Many of Kasper's points were taken up in the reports from the English and Welsh bishops, as we have already seen, and were reflected in those from other Western European hierarchies. This was to be expected, since Kasper is one of their theologians and his paper had been circulated among them.

When Kasper was named Secretary of the Synod, I wrote to ask whether when he wrote the paper he already knew that he would be Synod Secretary or whether the truth was the other way round: had he landed the job *because* of the paper? On 11 October he replied in English:

> You do your job as a journalist; that's okay. I do my job as a Secretary. Yes, secrecy can serve the cause of manipulation from within, but it can also prevent manipulation from the outside. So I hope you can understand when I answer your questions: no comment. Nevertheless I am content that you like what I say and what I hope to contribute to the Synod.

The importance of this reply was that it confirmed the accuracy of my presentation of Kasper's paper and his intention to work for these ideas at the Synod.

That Kasper should spontaneously introduce the word 'manipulation' into his answer – I had not used it – is interesting. Presumably the defence of secrecy as a safeguard against 'manipulation' from the outside is based on the idea that public opinion could seize the event and affect its outcome. But unless one denies any role for public opinion in the Church (and it was Pope Pius XII who first stressed its necessity), it was difficult to see the purpose of the blanket of secrecy that now descended upon the preparations for the Extraordinary Synod.

In mid September Vatican diplomats all round the world communicated the order that no reports or submissions from episcopal conferences were to be published. In Ottawa, to take one example, Archbishop Angelo Palmas, the apostolic delegate, said the Holy See wanted the Canadian report to remain 'absolutely secret'. The Canadians found this bizarre, given that the English and US reports had already been published and widely discussed. But Palmas said this unauthorized step merely showed that 'the norms of the Holy See had not been followed'. The Irish were poised for publication when the guillotine came down.

What did this new twist in the drama really mean? Were Basil Hume and the US bishops being rebuked? Had they made a preemptive strike, knowing what would happen if they asked permission? That bishops who are the *testes fidei*, the witnesses of faith, should have to ask permission to publish a text, makes nonsense of collegiality.

Then other questions came crowding in. How could one possibly justify secrecy about reports that were supposedly based on previous consultation? Those who had been consulted had a right to know what had been done with the material they provided; and even those who had not been consulted had a right to know what their own bishops thought about Vatican II. What had happened to all the brave words about co-responsibility that Kasper had developed so splendidly in his paper? How could there be involvement without knowledge, participation while everyone was kept in the dark?

The conciliar document on implementing Vatican II in the media speaks a very different language: 'The liberality which is an essential attribute of the Church demands that the news she gives out be distinguished by integrity, truth and openness, and that these should cover her intentions as well as her works' (*Communio et Progressio*, 29 January 1971 no. 122, in Austin Flannery OP, ed., *Vatican Council II The Conciliar and Post-conciliar Documents*, 1975, vol. I). Well, now this liberality-filled Church 'intended' to hold a Synod. This same document also has a highly relevant chapter on 'Public opinion and closer communication in the life of the Church'.

So the secrecy in the run-up to the Synod offended against both the spirit and the letter of the Council. Once again the fear that the Synod had been rigged gained ground. Certain Italian *Vaticanisti*, full-time Vatican-watchers, even reported that Walter Kasper had boasted of having already written Danneel's opening *relatio* (or report) in August. Thus the whole 'processing' of the sixty-eight replies became a charade, mere dust in the eyes of the public. I discounted this story on the grounds that it was altogether too cynical. But I could understand why this 'not-before-the-children' approach was bound to give rise to such speculations. What was there to hide?

In fact none of the banned reports – by this date a number of them had flown mysteriously in through the window and landed in a neat pile on my desk – contained anything discreditable to their authors, damaging to the faith, likely to 'offend pious ears' (a technical term) or insulting to the Holy Father.

For crystal-ball purposes, the most important of them was that from the Belgian bishops. Godfried Danneels is their primate and may be presumed to have had a big hand in its composition. As

Relator at the Synod, he would be the most important person present. He has already entered this story, but now is the time to introduce him properly. Born on 4 June 1933, he was therefore a youthful forty-six when he succeeded Cardinal Suenens as Archbishop of Malines-Brussels in 1979. Like Basil Hume, he has a reputation for spirituality. How this is acquired is always a mystery, but it has to do with the ability to talk about God naturally. 'He made the supernatural seem natural': Suenens' remark on Pope John hits it off.

He is also a hard-headed, practical, solid, methodical Belgian living in a country that stands at the crossroads of Europe. If Europe has a capital (howls from Luxemburg and the mayor of Strasburg!) Brussels is it. It is a city where the old and the new intermingle. It is wonderful and it is ghastly. It is hospitable and it is mean. The 'new poor' sleep in cardboard boxes under the motorways which carry the international *nouveaux riches* and the Eurocrats to their woodland homes on the road to Waterloo. Brussels and Belgium offer a microcosm of most of the contrasts and problems of contemporary Europe.

Danneels has been one of the leading figures in the Council of European Bishops. He accepts Pope John Paul's view that what post-Christian Europe needs is a 'second evangelization', though knowing perfectly well that such formulas resolve nothing. The point that emerged from the three-year-long discussions of the Euro-bishops was that there is still something for Europeans to do. In the past they had talked themselves into a corner.

Overcome with guilt for their colonial past, they explained that the future of the Church was clearly in Latin or North America or Africa or Asia – anywhere, in fact, except in Europe which was said to be tired, exhausted, played out and now entering a period of irreversible decline. One can deny this without falling into neo-triumphalism. Europe still has an irreplaceable mission in the Church which need not entail any form of cultural or theological imperialism. If Europe and North America cannot resolve the problems posed by the new technology and the third (or fourth) industrial revolution, it is unlikely that anyone will. The Hume–Danneels–Martini triangle (or Westminster–Brussels–Milan triangle) has made the Council of European Bishops a force to be reckoned with.

But Danneels is not a narrow European. On his return from Latin America in September 1984 he talked about the experience:

The thing that most struck me in Latin America was the struggle between life and death. You come across corpses of dogs or cats or donkeys, and the children play with them. In Bolivia I saw a man walking along a track carrying a dead baby in a shoebox. Then there is the filth clinging to everything. Everywhere, vultures, symbols of death, hovering over new life. And yet these people are not pessimistic. The Church is for them a great sign of hope. I saw no indication of secularization. (Quoted in *Cultures et Foi*, November–December 1984, p. 17)

A year later Danneels had not changed his mind. He went down into the lions' den, as it were. On 21 September 1985, he addressed *Communio*, the rival review to *Concilium*, which was celebrating the tenth anniversary of its Dutch-Flemish edition. Then on 26 September he said again that one had to 'take in' poverty with all five senses before pronouncing on liberation theology. True, one sometimes encounters along this road a short-sighted Marxism which makes the class-struggle the engine of history, glorifies violence, and dreams of a this-worldly paradise that has nowhere been realized. But that is not the heart of the matter, and Danneels regretted that Ratzinger's Instruction was so one-sidedly negative. Though it denounced a real danger, it did not point with sufficient vigour to an equally real need.

On Latin American matters, there is a marked contrast between Danneels, the pastor, who sees and smells poverty, and Ratzinger, the bureaucrat, who merely reads about it and, on his one visit to the continent, bravely ventures into a bookshop.

The Belgian bishops' report also reacts strongly against Ratzinger's pessimism. They list the 'fruits' of the Council as follows:

* progress in spiritual liberty and faith within a Church that has become less introverted.
* active community participation in the liturgical (and biblical) renewal and in the preparation of the liturgy. True of the Eucharist, but also of baptism, confirmation and marriage.
* increased co-ordination between bishops.
* the development of the permanent diaconate, welcomed by both priests and faithful.
* the growing involvement of the laity (above all women) in many of the Church's services, especially in catechesis and religious teaching, nursing, animating parish life.
* the progress at every level of a feeling of ecclesial co-responsi-

bility, leading to new forms of collaboration between priests and lay people.

* greater concern for adult catechesis, and the setting up of institutes and teams devoted to this work.
* the recent rise in vocations to the contemplative life and the flowering of new forms of consecrated life (secular institutes, hermits), of 'movements' (*Focolarini, Cursillo, Communione e Liberazione*), base communities, prayer groups and charismatic groups, etc.
* intensification of ecumenical concern.
* the development of a more comprehensive theology, more aware of the concrete realities of salvation-history (for example, in Christology) and more attentive to the researches of the human sciences (especially in family and conjugal problems).
* a greater openness to world problems, to social responsibility, especially to meet the demands of justice, solidarity, third-world development, peace-making.

This was a fairly typical list of 'benefits' of the Council that was being drawn up all over the developed world.

But of course Danneels and the Belgian bishops were not so naive or complacent as to imagine that no negative consequences followed the Council; but that did not mean they have been caused by it. In May, the Pope had told the Belgian bishops frankly that 'there are errors to be pointed out by name'. Despite this exhortation, they had to confess that 'we do not find formal or obstinate errors, but sometimes a one-sided emphasis on what is conventionally called "the horizontal dimension" of the Christian message'. There was an important shift of meaning in the move from 'errors' to 'a one-sided emphasis'. 'Errors' have to be denounced: 'a one-sided emphasis' can be corrected or adjusted.

However, Danneels and the Belgian bishops agreed that some Christians have undergone a crisis of identity: they do not know if they really belong in the Church or what they are doing there; or they transform the Gospel into a vague sense of human solidarity, benevolence and fraternity with the oppressed. So there can come a moment when Catholics find they accept the values of the Church but not the faith which props them up. Call this 'secularization' if you will, though the concept is confused and (they claim) increasingly abandoned by sociologists. They trace the process of 'secularization' at work in the abandonment of religious life or the priestly ministry, the drying up of vocations, the rarity of individual

confessions, the break-up of marriages. Danneels also concedes that 'the liberty' of the 'children of God', much trumpeted in the post-conciliar period, has sometimes been turned into 'an individualistic liberalism and a somewhat anarchic creativity'. One remembers the famous slogan of 'charismatic disobedience'.

If Danneels in his position-paper were to stress only what is contained in that last paragraph, then he could be skilfully edited to sound almost as pessimistic as Ratzinger. But these negative points do not cancel out the 'fruits' of the Council already gathered home. Having arrived at this same stage in the argument, the French bishops shrewdly remark that maybe there is a crisis, but it would have been far worse if the Council had never happened, for the Council was called to remedy the 'inadaptation of the Church to the modern world'. Like them, Danneels accepts crisis-talk, but he wants a better definition of it:

> The picture we have drawn reveals lights and shadows, strengths and weaknesses. The word 'crisis' is used in all its ambiguity: is it a crisis of anaemia, transformation or growth? All these dimensions are found in the present situation of the Church, with some regional variations. The Synod on the family showed that clearly enough. But hasn't that been true, though in different sociological conditions, from the start of Christianity? The Kingdom of God is always there, and not yet there.

Like Martini, Hume, and most residential cardinals, Danneels considered that 'unity in diversity' would be the main theme of the Synod. The primacy of Peter is unchallenged, he said, but its meaning is not always well understood. The relationship between primacy in the Western Church (of which the Pope is Patriarch) and primacy in the Universal Church has to be sorted out. Then we have a sublime example of the bland leading the bland: 'Recent controversies require a doctrinal clarification of the status of episcopal conferences, taking into account also the synodical tradition of the Church'. The only 'recent' controversy on the status of episcopal conferences had been that provoked by Ratzinger. This request for clarification was the deftest of velvet-glove rebukes to him.

The Belgian bishops' statement was dated 3 September – technically two days late. From 6 to 10 October Danneels was in Rome for a European bishops' symposium. This was a study session on the theme 'Secularization and the evangelization of Europe today'. It was called a 'symposium' to make it sound less threatening and more informal. Among the 120 persons present were theologians

like Paul Valadier SJ, Editor of *Etudes* in Paris, Johannes Schasching SJ of the Gregorian University, and Jack Mahoney SJ of Heythrop College, London. I mention these names to show that when the European bishops seek advice, they do not mind consulting those who have publicly trounced Cardinal Ratzinger.

Also present were Walter Kasper and Jan Schotte. In short, with Danneels giving a lecture and Hume in the chair, this was the dress rehearsal for the Synod. The three main actors were on view: the Secretary of the Synod Council (Schotte), the Secretary of the Synod (Kasper) and the *Relator* (Danneels).

A day and a half were set aside for discussing the Extraordinary Synod. One can easily understand that they turned eagerly to this topic when too much sociological intensity about 'secularization' proved wearying. A cloud was looming on the horizon: the meeting of cardinals immediately before the Synod threatened to make the Synod's debates irrelevant or merely academic. For the plan to 'reform the Curia' to be presented to it would lower the status of the post-conciliar bodies in the Curia, notably the Secretariat for Christian Unity. But that was strictly hush-hush until it was revealed in the *National Catholic Reporter* (25 October 1985).

This apart, the October meeting gave grounds for cautious optimism about the Synod. Ratzinger's pessimism about the Council was thoroughly rejected. And his negative judgement on episcopal conferences (and therefore *a fortiori* on groups of them) was neatly side-stepped by Cardinal Basil Hume in his opening address. He began with a concession:

> The Council [of European Bishops] has, of course, no juridical power over its members; it exists for the exchange of information and ideas and to foster co-operation between all the conferences. That explains and defines the scope of this symposium.
>
> It is noteworthy that so many presidents of bishops' conferences are present at this symposium. It has always been my view that the personal involvement of presidents is essential to the effectiveness of the Council of European Bishops' Conferences. It is only through them that individual conferences will begin to take action in the light of our discussion. (*Briefing*, 11 October 1985, p. 290)

Hume did not claim for the body over which he presides a juridical status that would have immediately been denied; instead, he laid down the moral conditions for its effectiveness. He was concerned not with status or juridical position but with what works. And no

one, however intransigent, can raise any principled objection to European bishops working together to proclaim the Gospel in their secularized continent. They were only 'exchanging ideas'.

In any case, Hume went on, adapting a theme of papal rhetoric, the Council of European Bishops' Conferences is one of the few bodies which span the present frontiers of Europe:

> In a continent divided politically and ideologically, our Council brings together its twenty-five members from East and West, from the Atlantic Ocean to the Ural Mountains, from Scandinavia to Malta. Our work together, our common concerns, our symposia, are a convincing proof that the bishops' conferences of our divided continent are themselves united within one universal college of bishops with Peter as its head.

In truth it is difficult to point to any other independent body which unites East and West in quite this way. Extend the same principle to the whole world, and one could say that the Synod would succeed simply by being able to meet.

So, having established the moral legitimacy of the Council of European Bishops' Conferences (leaving the canonists, should they so wish, to discuss its juridical implications), and shown the essential nature of the relationship with Peter, Hume then stated with the utmost clarity the responsibility of the European bishops themselves for the evangelization of their continent. They had this commission from Christ. No one could take it from them. It cannot be delegated. In a complicated but crucial passage, Hume explained why loyalty to the Pope as successor of Peter did not turn bishops into mere rubber-stamps:

> We are, in the words of the Council itself, 'vicars' and 'legates' of Christ (*Lumen Gentium*, 27). These are indeed noble titles. But it is at the same time important that we express to the Holy Father our loyalty and obedience, for these are necessary for the preservation of faith and charity within the Church. I believe it to be part of our function here to study more deeply the teachings of the Council on the ministry, both individual and collegial, of the bishops. . . This teaching of the second Vatican Council must, of course, be understood as complementing that of the first Vatican Council and not contradicting it. Pope and bishops have their God-given but distinctive roles, in the Church and in its mission.

Ratzinger had castigated those theologians who supposedly rejected out of hand everything that smacked of the pre-conciliar. Hume did not fall into that trap. Indeed, on his return home he had to rebuke *The Times* which in a leader had announced that the second Vatican Council had so convulsed the Catholic world that the 'old maps' to it were now useless. If by 'old maps' was meant earlier Councils, the Cardinal just did not agree. He was protecting his Roman flank.

Cardinal Hume's opening address to the Symposium, then, had the desired effect. There was no more loose talk about the episcopal conferences lacking theological status. For in his speech at the end of the Symposium, Pope John Paul said that the Council of European Bishops' Conferences 'represents a deeply significant and prophetic reality, and points forward to the way which has to be pursued with great conviction and courage'. So the whole discussion about episcopal conferences had been fuss about nothing. The spiritual reality of *koinonia* or *communio*, as it is actually lived in the Church, takes one well beyond what can be pinned down in juridical categories. So far Hume was doing well. The Pope had confirmed his judgement on a point of great importance.

The outcome of the next battle was more hazardous. Most of the emphasis had so far been on collegiality and *Lumen Gentium*. But Hume had this to say about *Gaudium et Spes*, and how the Council was related to the Synod:

> The Council helped the Church to move from an attitude towards the world of rejection and condemnation to one of openness, discernment and attentiveness to the 'signs of the times'. . .
>
> Some commentators claim that the Synod is an attempt, as they describe it, to change the orientation given to the Church by the Council. They seem to fear that a Synod can attempt to correct and redirect an ecumenical Council.

Hume clearly thought any such attempt would be preposterous: one simply cannot undo in two weeks what was elaborated in four years' work. So for him the purposes and meaning of the Synod could be simply stated: 'After twenty years, the Church must pause for reflection and assessment and rekindle enthusiasm for the study of the Council's teaching and its implementation'. That was his agenda, widely shared by pastoral bishops all over the world.

8

Senators of the Universal Church

And so to Rome on 20 November. Before the Synod could begin, there was a meeting of the college of cardinals. There was much overlap between the two meetings. Pope John Paul rolled them into one eighteen-day consultation when he said that 'the assembly of cardinals will be the authoritative introduction to the great celebration that will soon begin'. This suggested that the college of cardinals would have something solid to get its teeth into – finances and curial reform – while the Synod, as had been said all along, was more celebratory, more like one big happy party. I put this point to Cardinal Godfried Danneels at the first Synod press conference, but he stoutly denied any contrast.

What, then, is the college of cardinals? It is not an ancient body. Only in 1059 did it secure a monopoly on papal elections, never subsequently relinquished. From the outset the office of cardinal was attacked as unscriptural and untraditional. Five centuries later, the Reformation renewed these charges. Some of the churches that issued from the sixteenth-century upheaval retained episcopacy and therefore the principle of 'apostolic succession': none even entertained the idea of maintaining the rank of cardinal. 'It was never merry in England', roared the anti-clerical Duke of Suffolk in the 1530s, 'whilst we had cardinals among us' (Richard Marius, *Thomas More*, 1984, p. 359). The office was based on the legal fiction that the cardinals were 'really' the parish priests of the city who helped the Bishop of Rome (better known as the Pope) in the administration of the Church. So every cardinal today has the 'title' of a Roman church. Cardinal Basil Hume of Westminster, for example, has the 'title' of San Silvestro, the 'English' church in the heart of Rome.

For many years the college of cardinals had one and only one function: to elect the Pope; and though they may theoretically elect any Catholic layman, they have never in practice strayed outside their own 'college'. Sixtus V decreed in 1586 that they should not exceed seventy – a biblical figure based on some dubious exegesis; but Pope John XXIII in 1959 cheerfully departed from precedent with the result that by the time this meeting of cardinals assembled on 21 November they numbered 150. Some are very aged and infirm, and only 122 managed to make it to the Synod hall at 9 a.m. to hear Pope John Paul make one of the most important speeches of his pontificate.

For it was nothing less than a defence of the Roman Curia, and an apologia for his pontificate which he consciously set in the historical context I have just briefly described. This was a good instance of 'thinking in centuries'.

Three quotations framed the speech and gave it a vast historical dimension. At the beginning and end Pope John Paul quoted his predecessor, Sixtus V, the Franciscan Pope, who established the Roman Curia in something like its present form in 1586. So John Paul was saying that what Sixtus V did for the Council of Trent in 1586 he was now doing for the second Vatican Council. True, the intermediate stage of reform realized by Pope Paul VI in 1967 with *Regimini Ecclesiae* was acknowledged, and John Paul praised Paul as 'a lucid and penetrating connoisseur' of the Curia. But Paul VI had always intended to go further, John Paul said, and now he was finally completing the process of curial reform begun in 1967. Curial reform (though John Paul prefers to call it 'revision' rather than 'reform') is the last remaining task after Vatican II; for, as he remarked, 'the promulgation of the new Code of Canon Law, which I had the joy of promulgating on 25 January 1983, is in a certain sense the last *document* of Vatican II'. Therefore, too, the era of 'experimentation' is at an end – as John Paul has frequently pointed out in other contexts, especially when speaking to religious men and women.

The other important quotation was from St Peter Damian. Writing in the eleventh century when cardinals were still new-fangled, Peter Damian defends them on the grounds that they are the *spirituales Ecclesiae universalis senatores* (senators of the universal Church, *Patrologium Latinum*, 145, 540). This text comes from a period when the Pope was engaged in his lengthy struggle with the Emperor over investiture, and the issue was whether in the last analysis the Pope was supreme in both the spiritual and temporal realm. This had more to do with the development of Christendom than with the theology of the Bishop of Rome, but it led Damian to present the Pope as a 'spiritual emperor' surrounded by his 'spiritual senators' who therefore – and this was the point of the comparison – represented the true heir of the defunct Roman Empire. Yet in his *Paradiso*, Dante assigns his harshest criticism of cardinals to St Peter Damian:

> Their mantles drape their palfreys, so that then
> two beasts pace onwards 'neath a single hide:
> oh patience, what a load thou dost sustain.

(trans. Geoffrey L. Bickersteth, Cambridge University Press, 1932)

In the 1970s Pope Paul VI thought of changing the conclave that would elect his successor and assigning this task to . . . an Extraordinary Synod, because that would have been more representative of the universal Church, in short 'more collegial'. But he did not proceed with this plan. And his one attack on the college of cardinals – the exclusion of the over-eighties from the conclave – was bitterly resented. But it was a symbolically important move because it meant that there was nothing sacrosanct about the college of cardinals. John Paul's evocation of Peter Damian suggests that far from wishing to weaken the college of cardinals, he intends to strengthen it.

The very fact that John Paul has revived meetings of cardinals and given them some serious work to do proves this point beyond doubt. And in this speech he explained his reasons. To be a cardinal, he said, is 'not so much an honour as a service'. It expresses two aspects of the Church: its universality and its unity. That was why he called meetings of cardinals, explaining to them on 6 November 1979 that 'besides the task of *electing* the Pope, you also have the task of *sustaining* him in a special way in his pastoral solicitude for the Church in its universal dimension'. It was not enough for them to elect a Pope and then go quietly home, leaving him to get on with it: he expected them to back him up.

Thus while in the pontificate of Paul VI the college of cardinals seemed to lose out at the expense of the Synod of bishops, under Paul VI this tendency has been reversed. Paul VI thought the Synod of bishops was a better expression of *collegiality* than the college of cardinals, for a bishop has behind him a diocese, a local church, while a cardinal, as such, does not. John Paul evidently does not accept this line of argument. He takes the fact that there exists a *college* of cardinals to show that it is a *collegial* body. So it is, but not in the sense of collegiality *as defined by the Council*. For it says of bishops: 'Nor are they to be regarded as vicars of the Roman pontiff, for they exercise an authority which is proper to them, and are quite correctly called "prelates", heads of the people whom they

95

govern' (*Lumen Gentium*, 27). It is precisely because bishops are in communion with Peter and express the unity of their churches with him that *collegiality* in the strict sense comes into being. John Paul (or more properly the canonists who wrote his speech) does not accept this. Speaking of their present meeting, he actually claimed that *this* college of cardinals knew more about Vatican II than *this* Extraordinary Synod:

> It is interesting to note that out of the full complement of the college of cardinals [150], 89 were present at a part or all of the Council sessions. . . . They belong to the generation that breathed the atmosphere of the Council, and lived through the stupendous and generous, ardent and also dramatic period that followed as the basic Council documents were made known, diffused and applied.

But only a third of the members of the Extraordinary Synod had been personally present at the Council. Therefore, the college of cardinals was a better guide to the Council than the Extraordinary Synod.

But this is special pleading. First, because one has to ask not just who was present at the Council, but what they were doing at it. Some were physically present, but as members of the 150 strong *Coetus Internationalis Patrum* devoted themselves to defending the minority views that were eventually thrown out. And if only a third of the members of the Extraordinary Synod were at the Council, it was open to Pope John Paul to increase this proportion by using his right to nominate up to fifteen per cent of the total. He could have found room for Cardinal Léon-Joseph Suenens, for example, who, with the future Paul VI, was the principal architect of the Council. He would have been a better choice than the eighty-year-old Cardinal Gabriel-Marie Garrone who was allowed to reminisce on the first Monday of the Synod. Suenens who was present but without voting rights, did get in a few words later on.

Curiously, within the meeting of cardinals itself was the living proof that the college of cardinals is not as such an expression of episcopal collegiality. For the French Jesuit, Henri de Lubac, eighty-nine years old, whose contributions to historical theology have been prodigious, is not a bishop. When Pope John Paul wanted to make him a cardinal in 1985 he agreed, but only on condition that he did not have to be ordained bishop; for, he maintained, one should only be ordained bishop if one had responsibility for a diocese, a people – a principle that would throw the curial and diplomatic archbishops into disarray if ever they observed it. Since, therefore, de Lubac is indubitably a cardinal and indubitably not a bishop, this meeting of cardinals was technically non-collegial.

Apart from this concession to please the whim of a very old theologian, the relationship between the college of cardinals and the Synod of bishops has been tilted in favour of the college of cardinals. But the Pope also defended stoutly the Roman Curia. He said it was in line with the Council, and profoundly imbued with its spirit. He admitted that there were sometimes 'tensions' with local churches, but said they occurred only because 'there is an insufficiently precise understanding of the respective areas of competence'. But who is misunderstanding whom? That question was not asked, let alone answered, but one got the general impression that the Curia would get the benefit of whatever doubt was going. For no one can drive a wedge between the Pope and the Curia. The Curia, John Paul declared, 'is defined in relation to the Pope, and receives from him its authority: in its identity of views with the Pope resides its strength, its limitations and its moral norms' (*potestas et finis et quasi codex agendi normarum*). In short, John Paul concluded, it would be quite false to think of the Roman Curia as a 'parallel' body to himself. Thus he refuted a view that no one has held. The whole address was very defensive.

After the Pope had spoken, there were four other presentations (known locally as *relationes*) to help concentrate the cardinals' minds. They all dealt with controversial topics on which there had been 'misunderstandings'. Cardinal Joseph Ratzinger was top of the bill. We might have expected him to expound his views on episcopal conferences, but he sportingly left this task to his former deputy, Cardinal Jérôme Hamer. Ratzinger himself addressed 'Primacy and Collegiality'. He developed the idea that chapter 1 of *Lumen Gentium*, on the *mystery* of the Church, had been unjustly neglected at the expense of chapter 2 on the People of God. If one insists on the Church as *mysterium* one will not fall into the trap of seeing it in sociological or political terms. Mystery is the defence against democracy. According to the official hand-out, Ratzinger stressed that 'the Church cannot be considered on the model of secular monarchies in which the will of the monarch is the supreme law, and the sole source from which all power derives'. Whoever, at least since the days of *Pio Nono*, has propounded such a daft theory, was not revealed. However, Ratzinger also denounced with equal vigour the notion that 'the Church is a federation of particular churches whose unity is arrived at by simple addition'. It was, frankly, difficult to see why the *college of cardinals* needed to be reminded of such elementary points, unless (the thought did cross the mind) he was seeking to forestall the objection that the Holy Father was imposing his will on the Church (for example, in this matter of curial reform).

Next came Agostino Casaroli, Cardinal Secretary of State. Casaroli addressed himself to the 'delicate' question of 'the co-ordination of the dicasteries of the Roman Curia': 'delicate' is the Roman euphemism for 'controversial'. The problem had not been entirely resolved, he observed, by *Regimini Ecclesiae Universae* of 1967, when Paul VI made the Secretariat of State the co-ordinating body in the Curia. Its suggested replacement – the Apostolic Secretariat – will continue to have that co-ordinating function, but its main role will be 'to offer to the Holy Father that immediate and assiduous service of a Secretariat which is indispensable if he is to fulfil his duties of pastoral government'. The sentence is unnecessarily long and prolix, but the key word is *pastoral* government'. Despite all his years in the Vatican diplomat service, Casaroli was accepting the wisdom of taking the Council for the Public Affairs of the Church out of the new Apostolic Secretariat, whose function will be *pastoral*, i.e. not political.

Cardinal Hamer's treatment of episcopal conferences hewed close to the Ratzinger line, which was a little odd since in *La Nouvelle Revue Théologique* in 1963 he had written an article significantly called '*Les conférences épiscopales, exercice de la collegialité*' (November 1963, pp. 966–9). Hamer's conclusion was:

> The episcopal conferences demanded by the development of the world are not just a practical arrangement, but are truly a possible and appropriate manifestation of the solidarity of the episcopal body, a reality *de jure divino* in the Church of Christ.

It would have saved everyone a lot of heartache if Hamer had restated that doctrine: of course episcopal conferences are not 'of divine right', nor can they be, since there was a time when they did not exist; but what is *de jure divino* is the togetherness in *koinonia* of the bishops, which is *expressed* in the episcopal conference. But that was Hamer 1963 vintage.

The 1985 Hamer deplored the dangerous use made of the notion of 'subsidiarity'. He questioned whether this principle of Catholic social doctrine applied to the life of the Church. Since this is an important concept that will recur, I will give a brief account of its meaning and the debate about it. Found in the social doctrine of

Pius XI, the 'principle of subsidiarity' was addressed to the *state*; it was a warning – in the Fascist era – that the state should not interfere overmuch, and should leave to local bodies their legitimate autonomy.

It was a principle of political philosophy: the state should not do what a body on a lower level can do. Now it is perfectly true that one cannot transfer this principle without more ado to the life of the Church, for it would presuppose that the Pope was being treated as a stop-gap authority who only operated when the lower levels, say the episcopal conferences, called upon him to act. However, it was pointed out that Pope Pius XII in 1946 said that the principle of subsidiarity *does* apply to the Church 'providing its hierarchical nature is respected' (*Acta Apostolica Sedis*, 38, 1946, p. 144). More-over – and this ought to have been the clinching argument – the principle of subsidiarity is enshrined in the introduction to the new Code of Canon Law

After this preliminary softening up, the first item on the cardinals' agenda was a draft proposal (or *schema*) for curial reform. Officially, no one had ever seen it (though its existence was not denied), officially no one knows what the cardinals said about it, and offici-ally none of the conversations on which what you are about to read is based ever took place. Henry Porter's description of a day in the life of a lobby correspondent at Westminster described the Roman situation with total accuracy:

> He will attend regular meetings that never take place in a room that does not exist and will put questions that are not questions to a minister or civil servant who is not there. Between these briefings, as they are known, he may make a number of telephone calls which are not made and have lunch with a close contact he has never met. (*Lies, Damned Lies*, 1985, p. 68)

From these mysterious sources, then, one learned that the *schema* had been distributed not only to cardinals (obviously) but to Presi-dents of episcopal conferences and heads of Roman offices in July. Pope John Paul described this as a 'vast and highly diversified consultation' – a judgement that contains an element of rhetorical exaggeration. A round 200 is not a lot of people.

The draft was accompanied by a *relatio* which explained the proposed changes. The Commission that worked on the *schema* was headed by Cardinal Aurelio Sabattani. It is known that Mgr Giov-anni Marra and Polish Bishop Zenon Grocholewski – both members of the Disciplinary Commission – also worked on the text. So this was a reform of the Curia done by the Curia itself. It was a self-reform. Thus a chance was missed to have outside advisers – for instance residential bishops – who could have stimulated the Curia into an awareness of the pastoral needs of the Church. But that promising path was not followed.

The Commission was allegedly set up in response to the 1982 meeting of cardinals. Pope John Paul gave it the following brief: it should bring out the 'pastoral nature' of the Curia; and it should seek 'a greater correspondence between its own structures and those of the diocesan curiae so as to have more fruitful collaboration with them'. I transcribe this from the *relatio* without knowing exactly what it means. It can hardly mean that every diocesan curia in the world should match in its structure the Roman Curia with a mini-congregation for the doctrine of faith and a mini-secretariat for Christian unity. However, it does not matter much what this instruction means, for it was not carried out in the *schema* which reflects quite different concerns and priorities.

The biggest change concerned the Secretariat of State. It would remain the body in closest contact with the Holy Father, but its name would be changed to 'Apostolic Secretariat' to make it clear that it is in no way connected with political affairs. The *relatio* explains: 'The use of the word "Apostolic" highlights the close and special link that this department has with the person and the incessant activity of the Holy Father; and "of state" drops out because it gives perhaps a too worldly or bureaucratic impression that does not correspond to the reality'. But changing the name in this way would not make much real difference unless it were accompanied by another proposal which, this time, really is radical and dramatic.

Within the Secretariat of State Paul VI had set up the Council for the Public Affairs of the Church. It is responsible for running the Vatican diplomatic service, briefing the ambassadors accredited to the Holy See, and in general for all dealings with governments including those of Eastern Europe, for example. The proposal was that this body should be hived off from the Secretariat of State and become the 'Congregation for Relations with Governments'. It would thus take its place alongside the other dicasteries (as Roman departments are known). This looked like an enhancement of its status; but in practice it is not, for as Archbishop Achille Silvestrini, the present head of the Council for the Public Affairs of the Church, remarked with some vigour, the Council can be effective only if it is in day-to-day contact with the Holy Father. If it were kept at arm's length and worked at the rhythm of other departments (who can take two years or longer to prepare a document) it cannot *respond* to international events with the swiftness that is necessary.

It would also mean the downgrading of the whole Vatican diplomatic service; for if Vatican nuncios are no longer sure that they can have ready access to the Pope through this body, they suffer a loss of status and also a loss in efficacy. After a time they might peter out into insignificance. It is worth remarking *en passant* that Poland has got along happily without any Vatican diplomat since the war. One Vatican nuncio remarked that this division within the Secretariat of State would turn the Church into 'a soul without a body'. One sees his point.

English speakers in the meeting (one could mark them off because the proposals were debated in language-based discussion groups) did not have very strong views on the Secretariat of State: this was very much an in-house question on which old diplomatic hands, mainly Italian it must be admitted, defended the service to which they had devoted their lives. But the English speakers were deeply concerned by the proposal to turn the three Secretariats for dialogue – Christian Unity, Non-Christian Religions and Non-believers – into 'Councils'. These were all conciliar or post-conciliar bodies dedicated to *dialogue*. By far the most important is the Secretariat for Christian Unity which has kept alive the ecumenical spirit of the Council. In its twenty-five-year history it has had two remarkable presidents who became known and respected throughout the whole Christian world: Cardinal Augustin Bea, the German Jesuit, and Cardinal Jan Willebrands.

The proposal was that the category of 'secretariat' would now be dropped, and they would become 'councils'. Why did this matter? Because, according to the *relatio*, unlike 'congregations' and 'tribunals', a 'council has as its main task of study, promotion and pastoral animation and does not normally exercise any acts of government'. That this would be a downgrading of the Secretariat for Christian Unity seems incontestable – no matter what anyone says to the contrary. One of the great changes in the post-conciliar period was that the reformed Congregation for the Doctrine of Faith, concerned with orthodoxy, was balanced by the Secretariat for Christian Unity which was equally concerned with orthodoxy but also with the need to bear in mind the questions raised by other Christians. There has always been a certain tension between the two organisms, which optimists like Pierre Duprey have gallantly described as 'healthy'. That there should be a dialectic between these two approaches is no doubt a good thing. But now there will be no tensions, because the role of the 'council for promoting Christian unity' will quite clearly be subordinate to the CDF and also to the Congregation for the Oriental Churches. One should not look at this in too personal terms, but in effect it would have meant a victory for Cardinal Ratzinger and a big defeat for Cardinal Willebrands who, at the age of seventy-six, would surely feel the time had come to depart.

But that was the way things looked before the meeting. A reliable source reported:

> Last spring Cardinal Willebrands begged the Holy Father to change the Secretariat into a Congregation rather than a Council. Cardinal Casaroli replied in the name of the Holy Father that the matter could be discussed at the cardinals' meeting. (Luigi Accattoli, *Corriere della Sera,* 21 November 1985)

It seems quite extraordinary that Pope John Paul should have to reply through his Cardinal Secretary of State; it is as though he were unwilling to look Willebrands in the eye. It is equally extraordinary that papal permission should be required even to discuss the question.

Discuss it they did, and on the whole the meeting brought great comfort to Willebrands. The English-language group rallied round. It included Cardinals Basil Hume, Joseph Bernadin, and Tomás O Fiaich who all argued that whatever the intentions of the proposals, they would be perceived as damaging to ecumenism. The Roman canonists might claim that the Secretariat for Christian Unity was not being downgraded, but they had few opportunities to meet Protestants and did not realize that the most ingenious explanations would never persuade them that this subordination of the post-conciliar structures to the Congregation for the Doctrine of Faith represented a great ecumenical advance. It just could not be done, even with the most advanced verbal sleight of hand.

Ah, replied the protagonists of the project, but there is no longer the same need for a separate ecumenical body since ecumenism has invaded every corner of the Curia. If that really were true, then the Secretariat for Unity could indeed be happily abolished, its work completed. But it would be naïve to imagine that one can 'be ecumenical' without having any experience of the process. The 'reformers' – who on this point certainly included Ratzinger – made a better point when they argued that as ecumenism progressed, then there should be a closer link between the Secretariat for Christian Unity (or its successor body) and the CDF, since the 'conscience' of the Church was involved. But it was pointed out that the Prefect of the CDF was already on the board of the Secretariat. The suggestion was made that he should be on it *de jure* and not merely *de facto*. The most sensible solution would obviously be for the Secretariat to become a fully-fledged Congregation for Christian Unity. That would send out a loud and clear ecumenical signal.

Yes but, said the curialists, if the Secretariat for Christian Unity becomes a Congregation, then the same should also apply to the Secretariats for Non-Christian Religions and Non-believers, and *three more* Congregations would be administratively and financially unthinkable. The reply from the 'Anglo-Saxons' (who included Celts and Indians) was that this dire conclusion did not follow. The two other Secretariats were principally for study and dialogue, whereas the Secretariat for Christian Unity had a very precise practical task: to actually *bring about* Christian unity. Moreover, with its ecumenical directory and documents on ecumenism and the local church, it had already performed legally binding acts which, as a mere Council, it would not be able to. In all conscience and logic, then, the Secretariat for Christian Unity ought to become a Congregation, equal to the CDF.

But no cardinal was prepared to put his hand on his heart and say that this would actually happen or that the threat of reduction to Council status had been finally beaten off. The trouble with all Rome consultations is that *questa gente da fuori* (as the Romans call outsiders) eventually go home and cannot monitor what will happen next. In his 7 December address at the end of the Synod, Pope John Paul remarked simply that he was grateful for the advice given to the cardinals and that their thoughts would be 'taken into account so that the Roman Curia would be ever more able to fulfil its mission for the edification of the Church'. No one could read that riddle. The cardinals had asked for a deeper study of the *theological* meaning of the Roman Curia before the reform was proceeded with. It would also seem that morally, if not juridically, the Pope, having involved the cardinals in curial reform, ought to consult them again before proceeding to the next stage. But what is morally desirable does not always happen.

That maxim certainly applied to the tangled financial affairs of the Vatican which was the final item on the cardinals' agenda. But they were allowed only to hear about finance, not to discuss it. Finance is regarded as an area of special expertise that has to be

entrusted to the safe hands of a fifteen-cardinal commission. This
had already met 19–20 November to review the gloomy situation.
Its most influential members are Cardinals John J. Krol of Philadelphia and Joseph Höffner of Cologne, if only because they represent
the two richest churches in the world. Cardinal Giuseppe Caprio,
head of Vatican investments, anticipated the deficit for 1986 as a
record $56 million – an increase of $16.8 million over the 1985
deficit. One of the reasons for this decline is that the collection
known as Peter's Pence, taken annually on 29 June, feast of SS
Peter and Paul, was lower in 1985 than in 1984 when it reached
$26 million.

How was this growing debt to be coped with? Since the main
cause was the rise in Vatican salaries, especially of lay employees,
cuts were looked for in Vatican Radio and the Vatican Press. Some
Vatican Press employees have already been dismissed – to the great
distress of the Association of Vatican workers – and the possibility
that Opus Dei might take over Vatican Radio from the Jesuits was
once again evoked. The Jesuits would not be heart-broken at being
relieved of this chore which ties up sixty or so of their best men;
yet Opus Dei, though favoured by Pope John Paul, is not getting
everything it hoped for from this pontificate. They waxed very
indignant when *Civiltà Cattolica*, the Rome Jesuit fortnightly,
censored by the Secretariat of State, deplored their 'Byzantine'
methods of operation. But as a matter of principle, it was decided
that cuts should not be made which would impair the efficiency of
the Roman Curia.

Cardinal Casaroli then explained as best he could the affairs of
the Institute of Religious Works (IOR). It is not 'the Vatican bank',
he said for the hundredth time, but a bank *in* the Vatican. Last
year it paid $250 million to the Banco d'Italia to meet the conse-
quences of the crash of the Banco Ambrosiano, though this little
sweetener was in no way an admission of liability still less of guilt.
Casaroli pointed out what a good bargain this $250 million dollars
was. For if all the claims were added up, the sum being asked of
the IOR was a staggering $1,800 million. They could have gone to
court, said Casaroli, and it is not certain that the IOR would have
lost, but the image of the Church would have been gravely damaged.
So the $250 million dollars was a small price to pay for sparing the
Church unfortunate publicity. In any case, the money did not come
from the depositors in IOR – mostly religious orders.

Before concluding this chapter, I want to set down one of the speeches made at it. How can one publish speeches of a secret meeting? One cannot. But in this case, the author was so pleased with his handiwork that he got it published in the Spanish edition (only) of *L'Osservatore Romano*. On Thursday evening 22 November, Cardinal Ernesto Corripio Ahumada, Primate of Mexico, addressed Pope John Paul thus:

> Most Holy Father, in the name of a group of cardinals of Latin America, we would like to declare our complete support for the ecclesiastical service that you render by means of the Roman Curia. The church in Latin America is going through a time of great difficulties, especially in what concerns the integrity of faith. We take this occasion to declare our total adhesion to the *magisterium* of your Holiness.
>
> In this midst of these problems we are fully aware that episcopal collegiality only subsists through the strengthening of the primacy of Peter, who today is called John Paul. And we are grateful in a special manner to the Congregation for the Doctrine of Faith, for reproving the errors of a certain theology of liberation which, with the so-called *iglesia popular*, has caused so much harm to the faithful people. We are also aware of the dangers of the sects and of doctrinal and disciplinary deviations.
>
> At the same time, we recognize the grave social injustices of our continent. We are ready to do everything in our power to establish the reign of social justice, convinced that we will only obtain it by struggling [*luchando*] to preserve the identity of the Church. Nay more, to solve these grave social problems we need the help of the Roman Curia to keep the Catholic faith, sole means of attaining justice and peace. Only the authentic Church of Christ can convert hearts and take up the cause of the poor. May our Lady of Guadalupe help the successor of Peter to confirm his brethren (*L'Osservatore Romano*, Spanish edition, 1 December 1985, p. 8).

This manifesto – no other word will do – was said to have been signed by fifteen Latin American cardinals. It deserves a place in an anthology of the inquisition. For any Latin American cardinal who did not sign could be accused, would be accused, of disloyalty. Yet it would have been hypocritical of Brazilian Cardinals Aloisio Lorscheider and Evaristo Arns to put their names to a statement that positively *welcomed* the work of the CDF in their midst, imagined that denouncing errors was the most important priority for their oppressed continent, and substituted 'taking up the cause of the poor' for living among them. This smelt like a manoeuvre of Cardinal Alfonso Lopez Trujillo, the Pope's chief advisor on Latin American affairs.

But, as so often, the 'conservatives' put the ball in their own net. This posture of utter prostration at the feet of the Holy Father was not worthy of Christian bishops; the odiously exaggerated flattery belonged rather to a royal court than to the Church of Christ; and there was a dangerously totalitarian streak in the adjectives used (*'complete* support', *'total* adhesion'). It is statements such as these which harm the faithful and bring the Church into discredit in the eyes of the world. This revival of ecclesiastical Fascism made the Church, as St Thomas Aquinas would have said, 'risible'. It would be up to the Synod to gain ground after the painful impression made by this outburst.

9

Sing a New Synodal Song

Tutti a San Pietro! Everybody to St Peter's! The old rallying cry rang
out once again as the Extraordinary Synod began with Mass at
9.30 a.m. in the basilica of St Peter. The Council had started on 11
October 1962, with a procession of bishops wending its way in a
river of purple across the vast square; the Synod repeated the
gesture. It illustrated the idea, dear to Pope John XXIII, of the
Church as a 'spectacle to the world': these five-hundred or so black,
brown, yellow, and pink Caucasian faces, surmounted by mitres
worn at interesting angles or Oriental toques, said something about
the nature of Catholicism simply by walking across the square.
Catholic does not mean uniformity but 'reconciled diversity'.

Roman events are always marked by a battle of posters. First in
the field were the young people of the international centre for youth
at San Lorenzo. Their poster said: 'With the Pope and the bishops
to realize the Council'. One could not complain about that. But
before the paste was dry, another poster was placed on top of the
first, and it was of more doubtful taste. It invited everyone to a
conference on Fátima, the Marian shrine in Portugal where Our
Lady appeared in 1917. 'This Synod of 1985', it extravagantly
declared, 'is the last chance for peace.' So the Fátima adepts placed
their trust not in the meeting between President Ronald Reagan
and Mikhail Gorbachov that had taken place in Geneva the
previous week but in the words Our Lady is said to have
pronounced in 1929: 'Unless Russia is converted, the good will be
martyred, the Holy Father will have to suffer much, and various
nations will be annihilated'. But before the message could get across,
yet another poster was superimposed bearing the legend REAGIRE.
The furthest this movement went in explaining itself was to say: 'If
you want to react, come and join us'. Reactionaires of the world
unite. You have nothing to lose but your prejudices. The battle of
the posters reflected the ambiguities of popular Catholicism in Italy
and counterpointed the event in St Peter's.

It was 24 November, feast of Christ the King and last Sunday of the liturgical year. There were many empty spaces. The basilica seemed cold. The Sistine Chapel choir sang 'All people that on earth do dwell', which seemed to be one of the fruits of the Council. Why should the Anglicans have all the best tunes? But of course it was *Christus vincit, Christus regnat,* the ancient hymn to Christ the King (and signature tune on the glockenspiel of Vatican Radio) that soon took over. The procession took fully fifteen minutes to make its way up the aisle, accompanied by a vigorous litany of the saints. It was no different from 1962, when the Council started, or 1965, when it ended, except that many of the young priests of the North American College now sport moustaches. So far there had not been much applause. There was a whoop of delight when the television lights went on. Pope John Paul passed by, leaning on the pastoral staff he inherited from Pope Paul.

The Pope preached the homily. His text was the Gospel acclamation, 'Blessings on the coming Kingdom'. It was a straightforward sermon on the feast of the day, delivered throughout in Italian. The second paragraph (and that alone) referred to the Synod:

> We begin the *iter* of the Synod at this Eucharistic celebration with the same openness to what the Holy Spirit may say, the same love for the Church, the same gratitude to divine Providence which filled the Council fathers twenty years ago. During the next two weeks, all the members of the Synod, who include many who personally experienced the grace of the Council, will *set out together with the Council* in order to relive the spiritual climate of that great ecclesial event and in order to promote, in the light of the fundamental documents that were then issued, and in the light of experience which has matured in the course of the subsequent twenty years, the full blossoming of the seeds of new life sown by the Holy Spirit in the worldwide assembly, for the greater glory of God and for the coming of his Kingdom.

Towards the end of his homily, John Paul greeted everyone, especially the ten 'observer delegates'. This was a routine ecumenical gesture, that would only have meant something had it been omitted.

The Pope seemed more interested, one had to admit, in youth. At the end of Mass, he said, someone born twenty years ago, as the Council ended, would 'testify'. This 'child of the Council' would say what the Council meant for her. I missed her words, because of television duties. But outside in the piazza, after the Mass, as the sun came out, and the guitars of *Communione* e *Liberazione* twanged (they bring along their own microphones), John Paul told the young people that 'the future is in your hands' and quipped: 'Let us sing a new song in the Lord: the synodal song!' He sang along with them, bum-bum-bum, as they launched into some cheerful chant which sounded vaguely Latin-American.

Back in the inspissated gloom of the Vatican Press Office, the Opus Dei press officer, Joaquin Navarro-Valls, 'revealed' to the Italians (only) that the Holy Father would not give an introductory address on the morrow, that he would be present at general sessions of the Synod as far as possible, but that he would remain silent (*muto*) until the very end. This meant, he further vouchsafed, that the Holy Father wished to leave the Synod free to express its mind. I later met the Dutch writer, Michel van der Plas. He made an important distinction: in 1962 Pope John XXIII did not leave the Council free, he *set it free*.

It soon became apparent that this Synod, as it started work the next day, was unique in the series: it had no *instrumentum laboris* (working document) and only the sketchiest of agendas. The papal muteness meant that even more weight was thrown on the opening *relatio* (or position-paper) from Cardinal Godfried Danneels who himself declared that he arrived at the Synod not knowing what was going to happen. I believe this, because I think he is an honourable man. The full bearing of that remark will appear later. For the moment, the important thing was that the Synod, in the absence of anything else, would have to address itself to the Danneels paper. Without his *relatio*, the Synod fathers would have been like men pushed out to sea in a boat and ordered to 'Talk! Exchange information!' Danneels hoisted a modest little sail, evoked a puff of wind (of the Spirit?) and got the boat off the mud-flats.

We have already seen what he thinks. But here he was not speaking in his own name but collating and summarizing, with the help of Walter Kasper, the reports that had been received. In fact the main thrust of his remarks was unchanged. There was first of all a positive assessment of the last twenty years which contrasted with Ratzinger's pessimistic judgement:

There is a widespread recognition that an immense task has been carried out with courage and strength; though there have been disappointments here and there, they have remained within a climate of *hope*. There has been acceptance of the Council by the majority of the faithful, with resistance from a small minority.

109

Those outside the Church have become more interested in it. This understanding, though incomplete, was the work of the Holy Spirit in the Church.

At the press conference that immediately followed the morning session, Danneels was even more dismissive of Ratzinger. Asked to comment on whether a process of 'restoration' was going on he replied: 'The word "restoration" occurs nowhere in the preparatory documents of the Synod. It comes from elsewhere. We are here to have a Synod on the Council, not on someone's book'. After it was all over Danneels told me that Ratzinger's book had been mentioned only once in the Synod, by Cardinal Hyacinthe Thiandoum, Archbishop of Dakar, Senegal.

Of course they might have talked abut the concept without talking about the book. So we need to dwell for a moment on this 'restoration'. Its most obvious meaning is that of 'bringing back as far as possible a previous state of affairs'. This was attempted in Europe after the upheavals of the Napoleonic wars and was specifically known as *the* restoration. The Society of Jesus, having been suppressed in 1773, was *restored* in 1815. Of course in the meantime the world had changed much, and the *ancien régime* could not be restored exactly as before. Still, the aim of restoration is in principle to 'bring it back the way it was'.

Some writers have seen 'restoration' as the key to understanding the pontificate of Pope John Paul II. Thus Paul Johnson in *Pope John Paul II and the Catholic Restoration* (1982) compares him wonderingly to Mrs Margaret Thatcher and sets in parallel the way he set about cracking theological heads and the Iron Lady's brusque dismissal of the 'wets'. But Giancarlo Zizola in *La restaurazione di Papa Wojtyla* (1985) uses the term perjoratively, sees it as the betrayal of the Council, and compares the Pope to St Pius X who allowed a veritable reign of terror to operate against theologians.

Cardinal Ratzinger used the term restoration to indicate that he wished to see some pre-conciliar values like order and discipline reinstated. But his treatment is not exempt from ambiguity. For example he points out that Pope John XXIII 'approved' of the pre-conciliar draft of *De Ecclesia* ('On the Church') that was so brutally rejected at the first session of the Council. This is perfectly true. But the biographer of John XXIII may be allowed to point out that John XXIII also approved of the rejection of Alfredo Ottaviani's *De Ecclesia*, and liked what he was able to see of the new draft before his death. By now the notion of restoration was looking groggy. 'If it meant a deepening of the conciliar texts', mused Danneels, 'then it would be perfectly acceptable.' But one would have to be a conjurer to get 'deepening' out of 'restoration'. Danneels' predecessor, Léon-Joseph Suenens, gallantly tried to explain that what Cardinal Ratzinger had in mind was picture-restoration, as when one touched up an old master and highlighted the colours so that they emerged with fresh clarity. At this point the notion of 'restoration', battered and bruised, limped from the scene.

Cardinal Danneels called the four great constitutions of the Council the *Magna Carta* of the Church today. On this I owe the reader a *retractatio*. On p. 82 I said that Kasper's idea of taking the *four* great constitutions had been rejected in favour of the Martini plan for concentrating on the two concerned with the Church, *Lumen Gentium* and *Gaudium et Spes*. I was mistaken. I had assumed that the Martini plan would be followed *because it was the more sensible* and because the liturgy had already been revisited in October 1984 and pronounced in good health. There was another reason for keeping all four constitutions. Consideration of *Dei Verbum* on divine revelation would allow for a debate on the errors of theologians and lead to a call for a universal catechism or compendium of Catholic theology.

Though we were not to know it at the time (and Danneels said he did not know it), what he was presenting was the *first draft* of what would be the concluding synodal document. I will therefore give it fully in its first version, and discuss only how it changed later. Danneels, then, briefly summed up the positive achievements, constitution by constitution.

1. General consensus in the acceptance of liturgical renewal. More active participation in the sacraments, especially the Eucharist. The new order of readings has encouraged a broader and deeper understanding of scripture. The richness of the Word of God, especially in the scriptures, has penetrated the consciousness of the faithful. (*Sacrosanctum Concilium*).

2. The spiritual renewal of many groups as regards evangelization, catechesis and preaching. (*Dei Verbum*).

3. A more profound understanding of the Church, greater coresponsibility (deacons, lectors, acolytes, catechists). The 'base communities' constitute a great hope for the Church if they are truly Church. A dynamic ecclesial attitude has replaced a

defensive one in the prophetic mission and the missionary spirit. (*Lumen Gentium*).

4. A more profound perception of the relationship between the Church and the world. More radical testimony on the part of the Church in the area of human rights, justice, peace and freedom. Greater sensitivity to social problems. The preferential option for the poor, the oppressed, the outcast has entered into the Church's thought and practice. Positive dialogue with Christians of other faiths and non-believers. Efforts towards inculturation. An attempt to overcome the breach between the Gospel and culture. (*Gaudium et Spes*)

Danneels then went on to enumerate 'other points worthy of mention' and to conclude:

1. Bishops and priests – a better understanding of the office and the pastoral dimension of these ministries. Increased attention to the formation of seminarians and priests. Improved relations between bishops and priests, in fraternity and friendship. A more positive appraisal of collegiality at all levels. Increased awareness of the Church as communion.

2. Consecrated religious life: a great effort on the part of Orders and Congregations in rediscovering their founding charisms and in the updating of their Constitutions and Rules.

3. New vigour in ecumenism at every level: a fruit of the Holy Spirit.

4. Missionary spirit manifested through exchanges and collaboration between the churches, young and ancient. 'In our day a sort of new form of evangelization has arisen which has not been seen for a long time.'

'All of this constitutes a great motive for joy and gratitude throughout the Church. An objective vision, not to mention a vision of faith, authorizes neither pessimism nor resignation nor discouragement. The post-conciliar Church is alive, and lives with intensity.'

I interrupt Danneels here to point out how remarkably optimistic this part of his address was. Moreover, this summary of reports from the local churches, from what some like to call the grass-roots, embraces with enthusiasm causes which the Roman Curia had difficulty with, if not the Holy Father as well. That 'base communities' constitute the 'hope of the Church' is not a banal statement, since Pope John Paul criticized them sharply in Brazil on the grounds that the *parish* was the ordinary *locus* of the Church's evangelical work. Again, religious Orders like the Franciscans had recently been severely lectured and the Carmelite nuns were told to return to their 1580 Rule though they had massively voted for change: they would be encouraged by this commendation of the work they had done. The most remarkable statement is the comment on the 'preferential option for the poor'; for there had been a determined attempt to whittle away this phrase of Medellín and Puebla. First it became 'the preferential option for the poor and *the young*' (a big difference, since the young, as such, are neither rich nor poor); and then, in the Instruction 'On some forms of liberation theology', it was emasculated still further as 'a *concern* for the poor and the young' – a paternalistic approach which travestied the main point of this language, which was that one should be *with* the poor, not lecturing them from an immense height. Finally one should note that to say that there has been 'a more positive appraisal of collegiality at all levels' is very properly to broaden this notion and extend it to the life of the whole Church: it is not just confined to the relationship of bishops with the Bishop of Rome; but this implies that what is *juridically* true may not be what is most interesting or important. In all this the conclusion to the English and Welsh bishops' submission was realized: the point of the Synod would be to thank those who had laboured so hard for the implementation of the Council. Cardinal Hume was – to continue the metaphor at the end of chapter 6 – strolling home across the line.

There had to be a catch somewhere. It came in the form of the answer to the question about 'negative elements' in the reception of the Council. Again, Danneels presented what he had to say in terms of the four constitutions:

1. The liturgy: renewal often insufficiently prepared. Reforms ran the risk of remaining at a superficial level. In some priests a certain subjectivism has been noted; they forget that the liturgy is the patrimony of the whole Church, thus neglecting certain aspects associated with adoration, worship and sacrifice because of a certain 'horizontal reductionism' or 'moralizing cerebralism'. There is a crisis as regards the sacrament of reconciliation and the disappearance of many forms of popular devotion. (*Sacrosanctum Concilium*)

2. The emphasis on the Word of God has sometimes led to an isolation of the Bible from its vital context – living tradition. This has come about because of a subjectivism that tries to take the place of ecclesial understanding and the authentic interpretation of the *magisterium*. In some countries there are problems with the integrity and organic structure of catechesis. The gravest problem seems to be in the area of the relationship between morals and the *magisterium* of the Church. Many find it difficult to accept objective norms, and these are then passed over in silence. A clarification is needed regarding the relationship between objective truth and freedom of conscience. There is a risk of ethical subjectivism. (*Dei Verbum*)

3. Ecclesiology: the heart of the crisis. There have been unilateral, superficial and ideological interpretations of *Lumen Gentium*, especially regarding the concept of the 'people of God'. A tendency to oppose the Church as institution to the Church as mystery, the people of God vs. the hierarchy. This has at times created mistrust. There remain problems to be resolved: for example, the relationship between the universal Church and the particular churches; the promotion of collegiality; the theological status of the episcopal conferences (this point is often insisted upon); a desire to improve relations with the Roman Curia. (*Lumen Gentium*)

4. The relationship between the Church and the world is more difficult today than twenty years ago. In wealthy nations there is an increase in secularization, atheism, materialism and indifference, caused by the crisis of moral values. In developing nations there is increasing povety and misery, and the efforts towards justice and peace become more difficult. There are new problems regarding war, peace and the sciences (e.g. biogenetics). There are questions concerning the role of women in society and in the Church. In attempting to solve all these problems, one must avoid both over-simplification and extreme contrasts. (*Gaudium et Spes*)

The only comment one needs to make on these 'difficulties' is that none of them can be attributed to the Council itself. The last section indicates, further, not only that new problems have arisen to which *Gaudium et Spes* provides no answer, but that there should be a re-reading of the new 'signs of the times' with special reference to women whose role in society and the Church has changed radically since 1964 when this text was composed. In passing let us salute the old warhorse 'subjectivism' who was so frequently wheeled out at the Council. Of course the sort of 'do-it-yourself' liturgy that is sometimes found has its dangers, but it is not necessarily 'subjectivist' (i.e. a retreat into a solipsistic private world that pays no regard to the community of the Church). Sometimes the 'personal assimilation' of truth, which has to happen, is erroneously called 'subjectivism'. Danneels' *relatio* does not make that mistake.

A final comment on the negative section: what Danneels was presenting was not a sociological survey, and there was no reason for him to provide statistical evidence that in any case is probably not available. At the same time it would make a difference whether one says that these 'difficulties' are universal and constitute the most urgent problem facing the Church (which would seem to be Cardinal Ratzinger's position) and the responsible recognition that they exist here and there and have to be dealt with. But the fact that this section has to be read in the light of the first positive section meant that preoccupation with 'difficulties' need never become an obsession.

Still, 'remedies' have to be found. Here Danneels speaks with the utmost clarity: the answer 'cannot be reduced to disciplinary or administrative measures. Post-conciliar weaknesses cannot be put right by pre-conciliar measures'. To fall back on such measures is to be lacking in faithfulness to the Holy Spirit. Dialogue and 'the long patience of hope' are the way forward. If that means anything at all, it must surely mean that the disciplinary measures taken against Leonardo Boff must be lifted. For shutting people up is a 'pre-conciliar' measure. Danneels also called for a sense of history. Post-conciliar periods tend to be full of tensions. 'Without the Council, would it have been possible to avoid the bursting of the dam?' Danneels left this image and this question hanging mysteriously in the air.

It evoked the point made by the French bishops in their report: those who complained that the Council had produced a 'crisis' in the Church failed to notice that, but for the Council, the crisis would have been much deeper and more catastrophic. For the Council was an adaptive response of the Church to new needs that were placing intense pressure on its age-old structures. As Bishop Christopher Butler OSB once put it, 'but for the Council, the Church would have been like the Loch Ness monster – rumoured to exist, of venerable ancestry, claimed to have been seen by some, but not actually of much relevance to the modern world'.

Danneels' penultimate point was that what was needed was not a repudiation of the Council or even a revision of its teaching (for which a Synod was not competent) but a deeper knowledge and understanding of its teaching:

This is the common denominator of the responses. In this sense the Synod 'must not limit itself to being a thermometer that registers the temperature of the Church, but must also be a bearer of warmth to the Church'.

1. Generations change. Only a third of the present episcopate took part in Vatican Council II. Many of the faithful receive second- or third-hand information. There is a need for information concerning the Council to be disseminated through the means of social communication.

2. After the phase of post-conciliar fervour, there followed a certain disillusionment. The third phase will be one of balance, re-reading and recovery. We must therefore study all the texts as they relate to one another, without opposing pastoral ends to doctrine; to be able to join the spirit and the letter of the conciliar texts, because they are inseparable from one another; to respect the whole conciliar tradition of the Church, enriching it with the contributions of the present.

Conclusion: 'The understanding of the Council is the work of the Holy Spirit. The Synod cannot produce this new Pentecost, but it can prepare itself and invoke it'.

Finally, Danneels remarked that it would be impossible to deal with all these topics in two weeks. So their task would be 'to clarify the basic problems, fix priorities and provide an impetus for the future'. He offered the following four themes for reflection:

1. To examine more deeply the mystery of the Church in her vocation to sanctity.

2. To return to the sources: the Word of God, the living tradition, the authentic interpretation of the *magisterium*. To study better the relationship between scripture, tradition and the *magisterium*, and between the *magisterium* and theology.

3. To rediscover the richness of the Church as communion, especially under the aspects of universal Church and particular churches, and also as regards the theological status of the episcopal conferences. Finally, to insist on the communion between

bishops–priests; bishops–theologians; priests–laity; men–women; poor–rich.

4. The Synod must not focus exclusively upon matters internal to the Church; it must dialogue with the modern world. The liberation of man must be integral and embrace liberation from sin and death as well as the struggle for justice, peace and equality, all the while maintaining a clear understanding of the priority of the spiritual mission of the Church. 'For its doctrine and practice regarding this theme of the defence of human rights and of efficacious love for the oppressed, the Church is increasingly appreciated and respected by peoples and their political leaders.'

'The Synod must listen to what the Spirit says to the Church. It is a spiritual event, the work of the Holy Spirit. It must favour the fuller realization of the Church as community, her missionary impulse, her ecumenical dialogue and her total commitment to justice, peace and freedom for mankind. Finally the Synod must give to the Church a great impulse of hope in an era marked by so much suffering and so many negative factors.'

'With Mary, like the Apostles, the whole Church–flock and pastors – asks to enter the Cenacle. May the "new Pentecost" come, then, for our time, the "new Pentecost" of which John XXIII already had spoken as he thought of the future Council.'

After this lengthy speech, delivered in French, one might well wonder: what more was there to say? Danneels had anticipated, without dictating, the conclusions of the Synod. But there were still 163 members of the Synod who had the right to speak, and speak they did for eight minutes at a time. There can be no question of reporting on all the speeches that were delivered. It was a magnificent panorama of Catholicity. But it was very confusing as one was swept as on some magic carpet from continent to continent.

However a number of continental generalizations soon emerged. Danneels' analysis was widely accepted. The first world (Europe and North America) placed collegiality at the top of its agenda, and sought clarification of the theological status of episcopal conferences. Africa said the same thing in another way by recommending 'inculturation', by which is meant expressing Christian faith through African cultural forms (music, dancing, maybe marriage customs); Africans also complained about busy-body papal nuncios. They always do. Latin Americans invariably stressed the importance of

117

the option for the poor. In fairness, one must add that there was a very tiny minority of Latin Americans, led by Cardinal Raúl Francesco Primatesta, of Argentina, who denounced some 'popular church' at odds with the hierarchy and leading straight to Marxism. The second world – those under communism, who, Danneels noted, had been 'the most silent, the least explicit and the most discreet' in their responses – was joined by some Asian churches who are mainly concerned with how to survive. It was well put by a bishop who asked me not even to name his country for fear of government reprisals: 'You want to talk about the Roman Curia, OK; for us the most important question is whether we will still be able to say Mass'. So there was a multi-coloured map of the problems facing the Church.

Nevertheless, it became apparent with remarkable swiftness that this Synod had acquired a definite personality and was capable of having a mind of its own. No one was pessimistic about the Council and its consequences; everyone wanted to see a further development of the local church. The US delegate, Bishop James W. Malone, did exactly what he had promised to do, and thus delivered what Americans call ' a quick one-two' to Ratzinger's jutting jaw:

> The expressions of collegiality in the episcopal conference of the US are not just instances of those gimmicks and pragmatic contrivances for which Americans are thought to have such a penchant. We see collegiality as embodied in our conference as an important service to evangelization. How we relate to one another and work together as a conference does indeed reflect some typically American values and procedures. But wholesome values and procedures from our culture serve ecclesial communion and the proclamation of the Gospel of Jesus Christ, just as well as the wholesome values and procedures of any other people and culture.

But this was not just – or not at all – a declaration of American independence. It was a necessarily concise attempt to state why episcopal conferences have theological reality:

> Moreover, *Lumen Gentium* spoke of a collegial spirit or concern (*affectus collegialis*) which finds concrete application through groups of bishops working together (no. 23). *Christus Dominus* recalled the early centuries when Synods and Councils were established to carry out the universal mission entrusted to the apostles (no. 36). It spoke of an episcopal conference as a kind

of council in which bishops jointly exercise their pastoral office to promote the greater good which the Church offers the human race (no. 37–8). Thus some extension of the term collegiality in the direction of episcopal conferences seems warranted.

After that, one understands that Bishop Malone could enjoy his Thanksgiving Day turkey at the Villa Stritch, where Americans in the Curia normally reside.

There he might have bumped into Cardinal John J. Krol, soon to retire as Archbishop of Philadelphia. As President of the Synod, Krol was silent; but at a press conference he offered a somewhat more jaundiced view of the theological status of an episcopal conference. 'A conference of bishops', he carefully explained, '*qua* conference, does not figure in the hierarchical structure of the Church. . . . It is a useful collaborative pastoral instrument, but not an expression of collegiality, since collegiality always entails union with the Pope.' This came close to the Ratzinger position. The elected President of the US Catholic Conference must also have been a little chagrined to hear the other American specially nominated to the Synod by the Pope, Cardinal Bernard Law of Boston, urge that the Pope should get up a commission to write a catechism for the whole Church, since 'in a world that is becoming ever smaller, a global village, national catechisms no longer meet the need for a clear statement of the faith of the Church'. But if a national conference is incapable even of writing a catechism, it is not likely to be capable of teaching anything at all. So there was a clear contrast between what Malone said in the name of the US Bishops, and what Law said speaking in his own name. One suspected that he had been brought to the Synod to make this very point. It was a rather crude tactic.

There was no papal nominee from England and Wales, and therefore no one employed to shoot Cardinal Basil Hume in the back. Just before the Synod he had gone out of his way to say not only that he was not 'the leader of the loyal opposition' but that he never had been. It was the press that had invented this role and cast him in it. If there was a certain monkish disingenuousness in this claim, the earlier chapters of this book have already explained the reasons for it: Hume could be relatively laid-back at the Synod because he had done his work for it beforehand, and could now leave the limelight to others. So speaking on Wednesday 27 November, he needed only to declare his complete agreement with what Danneels had said on *koinonia* or *communio* as the starting-point for understanding the Church.

He tried to define it yet again:

> This word *koinonia* helps us to penetrate more deeply the mystery which the Church is. This concept means a gathering together of those who give themselves in faith to Jesus Christ and who receive the gift of the Holy Spirit when they are reborn by baptism in the risen Lord. In this mutual and virtual exchange between God and man, the faithful recognize their unity of life in Christ and their need for each other. In this description of the Church, unity and diversity exist at every level under the impulse of the Holy Spirit.

Note that what is being referred to here is an *experience*: the faithful have to *recognize* their unity in Christ and their need for each other. To those who say that the word *koinonia* is unintelligible to the secular mind, one can only say, come and join in the experience and then you will discover what it means. The Church is an original form of society, a community *sui generis*. That is why its style of unity is not reducible to any secular models be they democracy or monarchy or whatever. Thus *collegiality* is nothing other than the unique type of government that flows naturally from *koinonia*.

The Pope is the linchpin of collegiality: he is the only bishop who is the successor of a given apostle, Peter, who has the task of 'confirming the faith of his brethren'. The other bishops are 'successors of the apostles' as a group. This explains why *collegiality* is not a roundabouts-and-swings process in which what is attributed to the one is taken away from the other. It does not involve a demarcation dispute. Hume went on to explain:

> As a bishop of a particular church, I live in a profound communion with the Supreme Pastor of the universal Church, and under his authority, in a bond that can never be broken for it is of divine origin. It is an expression of that *communio* in which our particular churches are united in the universal Church. This has significance, too, for the relationships which should be developed between the bishops themselves. It gives rise to bonds between us which go beyond any sociological, demographic or institutional meaning of the word 'community'. Little wonder that it is often misunderstood by the secular world and not sufficiently realized by ourselves. The collegiality of bishops, when acting together with Peter their head, and when collaborating in

national, regional and continental meetings, must always be inspired and guided by an understanding of this inmost nature of the Church.

There were reporters who complained that Hume had 'said nothing' or 'said nothing new'. This was deeply unjust and superficial.

For Hume was expressing that *deeper understanding* of the Church that came *after* and *as a result* of Vatican II but that was struggling to come to birth in the text of *Lumen Gentium*. If the notion of 'progress' in theology were not ambivalent, one could call it progress – that 'leap in understanding' that Pope John XXIII called for in his opening speech. Since this was the real theme of the 1985 Synod, and since a 'deeper understanding of collegiality and of the theological meaning of episcopal conferences' was called for on all sides, the contributions of Danneels, Malone and Hume to this question took us to the heart of the Synod. And whether formally accepted in a final document or not, their thoughts would do their work and make their way in future theological reflection and ecclesial practice.

This is a large claim, so I had better substantiate it. *Lumen Gentium* taught us to think of different 'images' of the Church in the New Testament: it is body, ark of salvation, the Lord's vineyard, the bride of Christ, the new people of God, the pilgrim people. All these images express an aspect of the Church but without exhausting its virtualities. So they can correct and complement each other. But the preferred image of *Lumen Gentium* is that of the People of God. This 'image' had two great advantages. It said that all the baptized were members of the People of God and shared in a radical equality in grace; distinctions of office came in later. And the People of God also said that this people was on a journey, on a pilgrimage, was in history, and had to have a real relationship to each successive age.

But an 'image', however powerful, remains only an image: it points towards a reality but is not identical with it. And it can be misunderstood: People of God – as Ratzinger and others have frequently pointed out – can be understood in a 'populist' or 'democratic' sense. *Koinonia*, on the other hand, is not an image, nor is it a 'model' of the Church: it says what the Church *is*. Granted it is 'only a word'. But it is the best word we have. 'Faith attains', says St Thomas Aquinas, 'not the word but the reality [*res*].'

Now this pre-eminence given to *koinonia* is not just some advanced theological theory from first-world theologians. It is enshrined in the Code of Canon Law itself, promulgated on 25 January 1983. In his opening address to the Cardinals Pope John Paul had said that the Code of Canon Law was 'in a certain sense the final document of Vatican II'. Cardinal Rosalio José Castillo Lara, responsible for its interpretation, told the Synod that the new Code was 'the son of the Council, and tried to translate its ecclesiological principles into concrete canonical norms'.

The Code *defines* the Church as a *communio ecclesiarum* (368), a *koinonia* of churches, and says that the universal Church is realized only through the local churches (it calls them particular churches). In practice this 'communion of churches' is worked out through the special relationship with the Church of Rome (331, 349/3, 431/1). However the new Code omits one aspect that the Council has stressed and that one can legitimately restore. Being in communion with the Bishop of Rome, though the test of unity, is not the only form it takes; besides 'vertical' communion with Rome, there is also 'horizontal communion' between sister churches (*Unitatis Redintegratio*, 14). It is this which justifies the coming together of bishops of a region, or links between first- and third-world churches. This is explained by E. Correccio, an eminent canonist from Fribourg in Switzerland:

> In fact the setting up of provinces (canons 431 and following) and of local councils (439) is not seen as the result of bishops coming together in a private capacity, but is an emanation of the *communio ecclesiarum* which exists between local churches. (*La réception de Vatican II*, ed. Giuseppe Alberigo, 1985, p. 363).

The upshot of this argument is that those who try to oppose the 'juridical' to the 'theological' are making a mistake: they are working from the old 1917 Code of Canon Law, not the 1983 version.

Theologically justified and canonically grounded, the concept of *koinonia* has one further advantage. Cardinal Hume put it this way:

> The concept of· *communio* has been crucial to the dialogue conducted within the Anglican Roman Catholic International Commission. We have come to understand how we are part of a real but not yet complete *koinonia* or *communio*. This concept provides a context, too, in which the respective roles of Peter and the bishops can be understood and accepted without compromising the clear teaching of the first Vatican Council.

This was music to the ears of the Anglican observer, Professor Henry Chadwick of ARCIC-II. It would also have been noted with satisfaction by the Orthodox, for whom *koinonia* means the presence of the Holy Spirit. And the world ecumenical movement as a whole has moved in this direction with the Lima declaration on *Baptism, Eucharist, Ministry.*

The theology of *communio*, of course, implies certain structures for the Church, but it does not say what they are. If one thinks of the radical reform of the Roman Curia needed in the future, then the intervention by Metropolitan Maxim Hermaniuk, Ukrainian Archbishop of Winnipeg, may well turn out to be the most important. His starting-point was the unsatisfactory nature of the Synod itself. Since its role is merely 'to provide information and give advice' it can never arrive at a truly collegial act with the Holy Father. Decision-making rests in his hands. Paul VI, who founded the Synod of Bishops, hinted that one day, should the Pope so wish, it might be granted deliberative (i.e. decision-making) authority.

Thus Hermaniuk arrived at his startling suggestion. He proposed 'a permanent Synod of Bishops made up of members elected by the present Synod and others nominated by the Holy Father, which would have legislative authority to settle with the Holy Father all matters at present dealt with by the Holy Father and the Roman Curia'. Hermaniuk drew the obvious corollary: if there were a permanent Synod along these lines, then the Roman Curia would clearly be subordinate to it and it would have only 'executive' authority.

My first reaction was to wonder why Hermaniuk was wasting his breath: his plan would never get a hearing in the present climate of opinion. Had not Philippe Delhaye, Secretary of the International Theologian Commission, been spreading the rumour that Peter Hebblethwaite, a well-known 'conciliarist', was 'plotting to undermine the Roman Curia'? He had indeed. But there was no plot. Hermaniuk did not need any prompting. It seemed that he was merely brandishing the Oriental flag in proposing a model based on the experience of the Orthodox churches. Since the Catholic Orientals number a mere eleven million out of the world's 820 million Catholics, they do not have much influence. But their symbolic importance is great.

And in ten or twenty years time Hermaniuk's proposal will be there on the table, waiting for any Pope who wished to take it up. Hermaniuk invented a new 'tradition'. This matters because it seems likely that the Roman Curia, as at present constituted, will prevent any real progress towards Christian unity, not necessarily out of ill-will but because it was made for other things. Despite many changes of name the Congregation for the Doctrine of Faith is in continuity with the Congregation of the Universal Inquisition founded by Paul III in 1542. Its main aim was and remains the defence of orthodoxy. But one cannot be both defensive and in dialogue at the same time. So ecumenical progress demands a change of structures. No one so far has come up with a better idea than that of a permanent Synod.

Thus we reached the end of the first part of the Extraordinary Synod. The 165 Synod members and the token lay people – I particularly noted Virgil Dechant, President of the Knights of Columbus, who has been funding the Contras in Nicaragua – vanished into their language-based discussion groups on Friday 29 November. Though there had been some discordant voices, the Synod had began to sing the new synodal song called for by Pope John Paul.

10

A Touch on the Controls

Midway through the Synod Beethoven's *Missa Solemnis* was performed in the Synod hall. That stressed the mood of celebration, but one had a distinct sense of being taken for a ride – not some exciting roller-coaster ride, but a gentle ride. If one believed the English-language briefing, presided over briskly and efficiently by Mgr Diarmuid Martin, no one apparently ever said a good thing about liberation theology while its critics were expounded with some relish. The name of Leonardo Boff was never mentioned, although Archbishop Denis Hurley had told the Synod that if the principle of 'subsidiarity' had been applied in this case, great scandal would have been avoided. But Mgr Martin should not be blamed for this editing of the Synod. The same process could be seen at work in the chaotic Italian briefing over which Mgr Carlo Caffarra presided with increasing desperation, and in the lucid but curt summaries provided by Fr Jean-Michel Falco in French. So they were under orders from elsewhere. The result was that the world was given a picture of a bland Synod in which peace reigned. 'When I read the papers', Cardinal Tomás O Fiaich, Archbishop of Armagh, told Vatican Radio, 'I can't help smiling at these stories of clash and confrontation.' Irish eyes were smiling.

One of the reasons for this apparent harmony and tranquillity was that discordant voices were simply screened out. Liberation theology was barely mentioned in the Synod hall. Self-censorship was at work. It was treated rather in the way General Wojiech Jaruzelski treats Solidarity: not talking about it will make it go away. But Bishop José Ivo Lorscheiter, President of the Brazilian Bishops, and Cardinal Aloisio Lorscheider were allowed to lodge written interventions with the Synod Secretariat.

Lorscheiter tried to explain that liberation theology, far from being the work of a handful of way-out and audacious theologians, was rather the fruit of the pastoral work of the Latin American church as a whole. He carefully explained that liberation theology

125

'is not a theology of violence and does not legitimate violence. It is not a theology which takes up or appeals to Marxist ideology. It does not apply to Latin America concepts borrowed from European "political theology". It does not break with the tradition of sound Catholic theology'. He might have added that it renewed the tradition of the earliest missionaries in Latin America when, under the influence of great theologians like Bartolomeo de las Casas, the bishop was seen as the defender of the poor and the oppressed (that is the Indians) against the rapacious merchants and the brutal and licentious soldiery. Most objective observers of the Latin American scene accept something like Lorscheiter's account of liberation theology. One must be grateful that the Synod was allowed at least a brief and fleeting glimpse of the truth.

In a written intervention, Lorscheider also defended 'the Church of the poor'. The people of Latin America, he remarked, are for the most part rich in Christian faith but poor in almost everything else. So there are two reasons for listening to the people: 'They are a faithful people and a poor people, and as such they are loved by God with special predilection'. So the Church ought to listen to the people, and 'let itself be called into question by the message of the people'.

On Saturday 30 November feast of St Andrew, there was a press conference at which Dario Castrillón Hoyos, Bishop of Pereira, Colombia, and Secretary General of CELAM (the Latin American Bishops' Conference), tore into liberation theology with a violence that was unexpected in someone whose main claim was that he rejected violence. Asked whether he agreed with Lorscheiter, he replied:

> Yes, if he means that the Gospel brings a message of the integral liberation of man. But I disagree completely if he is trying to legitimate all the strands in liberation theology which have led to disorders and errors. We can never bless hatred and violence. I do not recognize a church with such goals as the Church of Christ.

This was in effect an excommunication of the church in Brazil. Castrillón Hoyos became even wilder as he denounced the so-called *iglesia popular* (popular church) which pretended to be with the poor, but was not, feigned to be with the peasants but was compromised with trades unions and political parties, turned the Mass into a political meeting, was an instrument of struggle at odds with the authentic Church whose aim was 'to grab for itself the *magisterium* from the hands of the Pope and the bishops'. One knew that Latin Americans were passionate people, but Castrillón Hoyos had surely gone beyond the limits of what is acceptable behaviour towards his fellow bishops. Theological disagreement is one thing; systematic denigration, caricaturing of opponents and demagogy are another – they are opposed to the principle of St Ignatius of Loyola that when one disagreed with another Christian, one should always try to understand his position by placing it in the best possible light.

Nor was this quarrel a Latin American sideshow way off the main lines of the Synod agenda. On the contrary, it was a vivid illustration of the conflict between those who asserted the *collegial* principle and the centralizers. The Brazilian claim was simply that they had *as a church* translated the Gospel in a way which brought some hope to their people; the centralizers alleged that this claim had led them astray. Castrillón Hoyos, like Cardinal Alfonso Lopez Trujillo, the Pope's chief unofficial adviser on Latin American affairs, is from Colombia. He is the Secretary General of CELAM. Its president is the Argentinian Antonio Quarracino, Bishop of Avellaneda. Both were present at the Synod as papal nominees. Both come from countries where anti-Marxism reigns. Both are 'close' to Opus Dei. It is not difficult to guess why they were invited: the whole sequence of events from 22 November when Corripio Ahumada made his obsequious statement to 30 November when Castrillón Hoyos launched his exocet against the Brazilian bishops was designed to dramatize the idea that the whole Latin American church is deeply grateful to the Holy Father and Ratzinger for the Instruction 'On certain forms of liberation theology'. There is only one thing wrong with this: it is simply not true. When one adds that the Vatican press officer, Joaquin Navarro-Valls, is a member of Opus Dei, it is possible to speak of 'rigging'.

This can be confirmed from another angle if we consider the fate of Bernard Hubert, Bishop of Saint-Jean-Longueuil, newly elected President of the Canadian episcopal conference. On Tuesday 26 November he had made two proposals to the Synod. This was unusual, for the Synod has no machinery for accepting proposals from the floor. Hubert said that the key question the Synod had to face – and the reason why it had attracted such immense press coverage – was this: 'Church of Christ, what message do you bring to this secularized world, and how are you living it out in your own communities?' His first proposal was that the Synod should send a message to the faithful and to all men and women of good will. Hubert was a new boy – otherwise he would not have made a proposal which was easy to make, difficult to carry out, and almost bound to end in tears. But it was accepted 'almost unanimously'. As Danneels remarked privately, 'Some people never learn'. But the Synod, which had already developed a mind of its own, would, it was hoped, have a voice of its own. In addition to advising the Holy Father – its main task – it would utter.

However, this announcement was accompanied by an explanation which robbed it of much of its appeal. The three President Delegates (that is Krol, Malula and Willebrands) decided to set up a commission of four – one per continent – to draft the message. One of the commission was Bishop Castrillón Hoyos whom we have just met. One cannot be accused of turning the Church into a democracy if one says that it might have been better if the Synod had been allowed to elect its own drafting committee. But that could not be done, said Cardinal Joseph Malula at a press conference, because 'the Church is a mystery'. This was the favourite theme of Cardinal Ratzinger. But the only mystery here was who was controlling the Synod. None of this mattered in the slightest for Cardinal Jean-Marie Lustiger of Paris was appointed to write the text. He threw himself into the work with zest, produced what he called 'a biblical exhortation' in a style so appalling that French Cardinal Roger Etchegaray squirmed with embarrassment as Lustiger perorated. Danneels later said that Lustiger's text was a fine piece of rhetoric but it had nothing to do with the work of the Synod. He noted that one synodal father had said, '*Hoc non mihi placet*' ('I don't like this at all') while the usual polite formula was '*Mihi placet, sed. . .*' ('I like it, but . . .'). It was written in Gallic message style: 'In a world torn by strife, division etc., the Synod proclaims, yet again, the Church's message of peace, hope, justice, reconciliation etc'. Lustiger's message was leaked by *Agence France Presse* and appeared on page one of *Le Monde*. It was then very properly forgotten.

Hubert's second proposal was more far-reaching. Granted that, as Danneels had said in his opening *relatio*, it was impossible to deal in a mere two weeks with all the highly important questions that had been raised:

> Why not use this time to identify the problems which the Synod wishes to tackle and then adjourn until next year or even later? This would allow the Synod fathers to return home to discuss these topics with the members of their respective episcopal confer-

ences. Thus all the bishops could share in this experience of this Synod with us.

And thus, one might add, all the bishops of the world would spiritually gather round the Holy Father and perform an act that even Cardinal Ratzinger would have to acknowledge as truly collegial (*vere collegialis*). At dinner the next night I put it to Hubert that his proposal was doomed. The Synod Secretariat held that a Synod ceased to exist when it came to an end, and that there was no continuity from one Synod to the next, 'Well', he said, with new-world optimism, 'let's change the rules.'

That did not seem very likely. Yet Hubert's unsuccessful proposal contained a rider that was, in the strictest sense of the term, 'prophetic'. If the bishops took home a list of topics for discussion, then:

This would also give the opportunity for all the baptized, who so desire, to take an active part in the life of the universal Church. Lay women and men, religious and priests are all responsible with us for the mission of Christ entrusted to the Church. They are thus active participants and have a stake in the actions resulting from Vatican II. They too have received the Spirit of God to guide them in their apostolic witness. If the present Synod were to become the first step in a two-year process, the work which we are now beginning could become the occasion of a consultation with the faithful, of a genuine participation on their part, of the 'missioning' of a large number of Christians mandated with us to shed light on how particular points of Vatican II have been received. This process would give to each of the faithful the possibility of making the message of the Church more believable. The Church is the People of God, the Body of Christ, the Temple of the Holy Spirit. To the degree that the members participate in a responsible way in all aspects of the life of this Church, it will become ever more the sign of salvation. As Christ gave witness to the truth of God and of man, through his way of life, so the Church today must give account to the truth of women and men called to live in society, by the way in which she helps her members to grow together and to face their daily difficulties.

This visionary proposal was not discussed, not 'received'. It remained just a bright idea, a twinkle in the eye of the Bishop of Saint-Jean-Longueuil, a firework that dazzled briefly and soon fizzled out. It remains to add that the Vatican press office provided no summary of this intervention, and that when Hubert complained mildly, he was told that his manuscript had been 'lost'. But it was already circulating in *samizdat* form.

The most important part of the Synod then took place invisibly, inaudibly and behind closed doors. There were nine language-based discussion groups. It was said that the groups had elected their own chairmen and secretaries. In that case, the two English-language groups looked distinctly promising for Cardinals Basil Hume and Francis Arinze renewed the partnership that had been so fruitful in the cardinals' meeting, while Cardinal Tomás O Fiaich presided over the group whose secretary was Bishop James W. Malone. The other presidents and secretaries will be mentioned later. What were they supposed to be discussing in the ten hours they had available between Friday and Monday?

Officially they were discussing a second edition of Danneel's original *relatio*. It now became clear that this was a draft for the final document of the Synod. Reporters were given only a summary of this new *relatio*. It raised the question: what had happened to the Danneels who had started the Synod so magnificently only four days previously? He now appeared to think that 'the relationship between theologians and the *magisterium* of the bishops' was a most urgent question, and that 'the birth and spread of sects poses the problem of responding to the spiritual hunger of contemporary man'. And the Danneels who said one had to smell poverty in order to understand it now relapsed into indigestible abstractions such as 'the rightful autonomy of human culture must be distinguished from an autonomist vision of man and the world which casts aside and denies spiritual values'. It was all very puzzling.

It is true, however, that there was a section on the Church as *communio* on which one could begin to build. There were promising hints about collegiality. But even this section ended with sinister remarks about episcopal conferences: 'There is no doubt about their utility, indeed their pastoral necessity. But they are based on ecclesiastical law' – that is, *only* based on canon law. This was the Ratzinger thesis.

But this negative judgement on the second *relatio* was based on the hand-out provided by the Vatican press office. When, two days later, I was able to read the full text of Danneel's remarks, it was evident that the official summary had distorted the plain meaning of the text. For example, the Danneels report, after noting the stress on *communio*, went on:

Collegiality is a reality with a basis in the sacraments; therefore the collegial spirit covers a far wider field than the mere juridical exercise of collegiality. In so far as it is a sacramental reality, it cannot be reduced to mere debate about consultative or deliberative status. This must not be lost sight of when we talk of improving the Synod of Bishops.

Nor were episcopal conferences dismissed so scurvily:

No one could doubt the pastoral usefulness, indeed the necessity in today's circumstances, of episcopal conferences. We are further agreed in recognizing in them a clear expression and concrete realization of the bond of collegiality (see *Lumen Gentium*, 23). Their existence, however, is based on ecclesiastical law.

Put that way, it was a mere truism, not a weapon directed at their very existence. I do not know why the Vatican press office turned a good document into a wretched one; it might have been due to incompetence rather than villainy, or perhaps they have just got into the habit of not being straightforward.

For all I know, the discussions may have proceeded with that urbanity and serenity that everyone said was breaking out on all sides now that the groundlings of the press had been locked out. However, it is a reasonable guess that the Spanish-language group A had some rather animated discussions. For its President was Cardinal Eugenio de Araújo Sales of Rio de Janeiro. While the Africans thought of the Church on the model of the family, Cardinal Ratzinger pressed the claims of mystery and the other Europeans the concept of *koinonia*, Sales presented a police-force model of the Church. Using a homely analogy he said that the state sees to it that poisonous goods are not sold in the shops. But the Church lets poisonous matter be hawked around without anyone lifting a finger to stop it. 'Grave errors are abroad', he declared, 'that are sometimes taught in seminaries and theological schools, and the people and the seminarians are not protected from them.' What was to be done about those who taught 'grave moral and dogmatic errors'? Sales recommended 'the suspension or replacement of such professors' and 'apostolic visitations followed by practical consequences'. By practical consequences. Sales meant sackings. He had already set an example by firing Clodovis Boff, brother of Leonardo. He also denounced religious generally 'who lacked respect for the Holy Father and even opposed the Roman Curia'.

Lorscheider is a Franciscan. In Spanish-language group A he

and Ivo Lorscheiter were under the presidency of Sales, who was said to have been 'elected' by the group. This reversal of roles was ironical, because in Brazil Lorscheiter is the properly elected President of the episcopal conference of which Sales is an unruly member. Also in the group was the passionate Colombian, Castrillón Hoyos, who could be relied upon to keep an eye on things. He knew that the famous 'positive document' on liberation theology was due out soon. He had won.

The next decisive date was 3 December, feast of St Francis Xavier, when the nine *circuli minores* (as they were called) were due to report back. A first reading of their efforts produced a sense of incoherence. The Italian group was presided over by Cardinal Ugo Poletti, Vicar of Rome and the papal choice as President of the Italian Bishops' Conference; but Cardinal Silvio Oddi, Prefect of the Congregation for the Clergy, insisted on hogging the floor. So they ended up recommending that the sabbath should be kept holy and that a compendium on moral questions, to which everyone would have to conform, should be composed by the Holy See.

The Spanish-language group A, from which so much passionate intensity had been expected, appeared to have buried the hatchet (and no doubt marked the spot). Cardinal Sales did not get all his own way. There was some difficult code-language (translation in brackets). 'The salvific value of suffering must be acknowledged' (the poor have to accept their lot). 'The Church is not only a people but a sign of the unity of the whole human race' (the rich have souls too). 'The Roman Curia is involved in the communion of the Church' (one cannot contrast a proper bishop in his diocese with a curial bishop without a diocese). 'We do not think a concluding document is needed for Synod meetings have a value in themselves' (we were unable to reach agreement). Finally, in a prophetic burst, they denounced the arms trade and the building up of arsenals of war.

The French groups A and B talked at inordinate length about 'secularization'. They agreed it was not caused by Vatican II. They further opined that it was *positive* if it meant a release from false pieties but *negative* if it meant doing without God. But that platitude raises a very 'European' question, and they had many Africans in their midst who said one should not speak of 'fetishism', a term that was injurious and inaccurate. They denounced 'false feminist claims' (though what they would have done with 'genuine feminist claims' one does not know). They, too, called for a doctrinal and moral compendium for the universal Church, without explaining how it would be written. Enough. I will come to the two English-language groups in a moment, pausing only to say that the ten forlorn individuals who insisted on talking Latin to each other contributed nothing but alarm and despondency. Cardinal Pietro Palazzini, who favours the canonization of *Pio Nono*, was their distinguished President.

The German group was presided over by Cardinal Joseph Höffner of Cologne, whose financial expertise is not in doubt. It included some of the most liberal-minded members of the Synod – retired Bishop John W. Gran of Oslo, Cardinal Stephen Sou Hwan Kim of Seoul, Cardinal Jan Willebrands of the Secretariat/Council/Congregation for Christian Unity, not to mention his successor in Utrecht, Cardinal Adriaan Simonis. It is true that the German group also included former members of the Austro-Hungarian Empire such as Cardinal Frantisek Tomasek, Prague, Archbishop Jerzy Stroba from Poznan, Poland, and the inimitable Cardinal Laszlo Lekai of Esztergom, Hungary, who had invited everyone to Budapest for the hundredth anniversary of the death of the composer Franz Liszt. Liszt, he observed, though only in minor orders, did not mind wearing clerical dress; he did not add that other aspects of Liszt's sentimental life ('He dragged his bleeding heart across Europe') were somewhat less than exemplary for young clerics. Lekai must be a great disappointment to Pope John Paul II who once quoted the proverb: 'When Poles and Hungarians meet, they either fight each other or drink together'. But here was Lekai going on about Liszt and not being in the least heroic; indeed he claimed that the fact that Hungarian Radio announced the saint of the day every morning was an important and little recognized blow to secularization. I list the German speakers merely to make the point that, despite their colourful diversity, the only voice that came through in their report was that of Cardinal Joseph Ratzinger, who obviously intimidated them by the sheer prestige of his office.

The German-language group, then, declared that the Church was a *mysterium*. They wondered about the prevalence and causes of the *anti-Römische-Effekt* – a phrase of Hans Urs von Balthasar which means roughly 'anti-Roman prejudice' and is exhibited, in exemplary form, by Hans Küng. I do not say this is true, but it is what these people believe. They said that some had invented a 'do-it-yourself' Church, that we neglected the witness of the saints, and that we have talked too much about the Church and not enough about Christ. (They did not obey their own maxim.) Many Christians feel, they averred, that their Christian inheritance is being

133

frittered away. Individual conscience has been exalted above objective moral norms. Theological weaknesses must be corrected. The values of holiness, silence, prayer and adoration must be restored to the Church. Collegiality only existed in an ecumenical Council, and every other use of the term was derived and analogous. Bishops' conferences are useful, but they should not usurp the responsibility of the individual bishop. The Holy Father was thanked for making the *ad limina* visits – the five-yearly personal report to Rome that every bishop must make – a vital part of his ministry. Though Cardinal Ratzinger hid his light under a bushel and allowed Cardinal Augustin Mayer, Prefect of the Congregation for Divine Worship, graciously to act as *rapporteur*, every single theme developed by him came from *The Ratzinger Report* (by now it had been translated). It might also be observed that Mayer's remarks answered none of the questions put in the Danneels report. At this point the papal silence and the lack of clarity about the aim of the Extraordinary Synod made it very difficult, if not impossible, to conclude at all. There were only three more working days to go.

English-language group A, the Hume–Arinze team, which contained many Africans, agreed on *koinonia* and drew out its implications for the involvement of lay women and men in 'pastoral reflection and decision-making processes'. The presence of many Africans and Asians was reflected in its stress on 'inculturation' – the adaptation of Christian faith to different cultures, though the statement of it was strictly tautological: 'That inculturation compatible with the message of Christ be encouraged'. But the debate is precisely about at what point it becomes incompatible with the message of Christ. And surprisingly, only two members rallied to the 'high' collegial view of episcopal conferences, while ten members wished to emphasise rather that 'the episcopal conferences are designed to support and not to replace or to diminish the responsibility of individual bishops'. Coming from this group, this was a surprising and rather rash judgement, since there can be no serious 'inculturation' without a strong and cohesive episcopal conference: an individual bishop cannot walk alone down this road.

But the main recommendation of the English-speaking group A was practical. If the Holy Father was to produce a document based on the recommendations of the Synod, then 'the earlier such a document is issued, the greater its effect is likely to be, because this Synod will remain fresh in people's memories'. This was a polite way of saying that an apostolic exhortation which appeared in six months' time might well be a lead balloon. The group also toyed with the idea of another Synod in 1990, twenty-five years after Vatican II, that would prepare the way for an intensive 'call to action' in the last decade of the century. These ideas might well appeal to Pope John Paul who, if still alive, will be eighty in the year 2,000. But it looks as though efficient lobbying has already fixed 'the Word of God' as the theme of the 1990 Synod.

There was a brief ecumenical interlude on Tuesday 3 December when Professor Henry Chadwick spoke in the name of the ten ecumenical observers who came from the churches or bodies with whom a theological dialogue has been engaged. Chadwick, an Anglican, was standing in for Mark Santer, Bishop of Kensington, who had a slipped disc. As a member of the Anglican Roman Catholic International Commission, Chadwick naturally rejoiced at the way *koinonia* was becoming a key concept:

> These episcopal conferences and other collegial structures at local and parochial level are significant for ecumenism in enhancing the possibilities of co-operation. The emphasis placed, both at Vatican II and in this Synod, on communion (*koinonia*) as a key to the understanding of the nature of the Church is important for ecumenism. This communion is created for us, not by us: it draws us to the Father in Christ through the Holy Spirit.

Chadwick also had some advice on ecumenical method:

> Notwithstanding doctrinal differences which still exist, some questions which were once divisive have come in time to be seen in a different perspective, not now as church-dividing questions. We all need to learn how to take account of these new insights and act upon them so that the divisions of the Church may be healed, and also that new difficulties are not created.

This might have been construed as a delicate rebuke to Ratzinger who said that ARCIC ought to have compared sixteenth-century formulations of doctrines in the Council of Trent and the Thirty-Nine Articles. But Chadwick has always maintained that one should 'get behind the sterile Maginot Line of past controversies in order to discuss the living faith of today'. However, with the remark about 'not creating new difficulties', he looked over his shoulder at those Anglicans who have ordained women as priests. But he was not making an 'Anglican' point: the whole ecumenical movement has to use this method, and start from what the Spirit is saying to the Churches *now*. Professor Chadwick was applauded. Quite right too. An ecumenism that knows its place is a good thing.

The next applause in the Synod came on the evening of Friday 6 December, when Cardinal Godfried Danneels' absolutely final report was read out. One must suppose that the applause was due to a feeling that the end was in sight, and that the Synod would have something to show – a sixteen-page Latin document – for its labours. But a calm reading of the text made it clear that this was not wholly the work of Danneels. Whatever the Spirit may have been saying to the churches, someone else had got at Danneels. For the report reflected, point by point, what the German-language group had said; the other eight were used only to the extent that they confirmed the German-language positions. Had this text been prepared in advance? Was this the answer the Synod had been programmed to give from the outset? I believe that it was, and that thus Pope John Paul would be able to endorse it with enthusiasm and rejoice that the Synod had so accurately summed up his own views.

The opening paragraph contains the tell-tale observation that Synod was able to share in 'the joys and the hopes, the griefs and anxieties which the *churches* scattered throughout the world often experience'. That is what the Pope had said in his 25 January address. Already one noted his significant adaptation of the opening chord of *Gaudium et Spes* which shares in 'the joys and the hopes, the griefs and the anxieties *of the men of this age, especially those who are poor or in any way afflicted*'. This change means that the Church has become more introverted.

The 'world' is now seen as a much more dangerous place. Secularism, consumerism, and immanentism show – says the report – that 'the Prince of this world' and the 'mystery of iniquity' are still at work in our age. This completes the papal 'revision' of the optimism of *Gaudium et Spes*. We saw in chapter 2 that Karol Wojtyla never really liked it. So now he rewrites it. The report also contains a typical contrast between the different 'worlds':

> Particularly with regard to the first world we have to ask why after a full and profound exposition of the doctrine of the Church there should be so much disaffection towards the Church, even where the fruits of the Council abound. But where the Church is oppressed by a certain totalitarian ideology or where she speaks out against social injustice, she seems to be accepted much more readily. Yet even there it has to be admitted that there is not among all the faithful a full and complete identification with the primary mission of the Church (no. 3).

The last sentence is a veiled attack on liberation theology.

So there is nothing new in this document. 'Theologians' reappear once more as people who 'sow confusion among the faithful': there is no acknowledgement of the English and Welsh bishops' insight that the confusion came about because of the simplistic versions of Christianity previously presented to the faithful. So instead of the stimulating collaboration between bishops and theologians such as is found in the Council of European Bishops, we are invited to return to an era of cat-and-mouse suspicion in which ever-vigilant bishops 'strengthen the faith of the flock, and ward off dangers'. Apropos, there is a curious and unsubstantiated distinction between 'pluriformity' and 'pluralism'. Reference is made to *Lumen Gentium*, 23, which is alleged to make this distinction: 'Since pluriformity brings with it a true enrichment and fullness, it is true catholicity: however, a pluralism of opposite views leads to collapse, ruin and loss of identity'. *Alice in Wonderland* again: 'Words can mean anything I say they mean'.

This distinction naturally affects the discussion of collegiality which, however, makes some gestures towards the synodal discussions. But it ominously recalls the *Nota Praevia* (see p. 60 above) which says that the college never exists without its head, and it includes the Roman Curia and *ad limina* visits when bishops come to Rome to receive their marching orders among the 'instruments of collegiality'; the others are the Synod of Bishops and episcopal conferences.

Episcopal conferences do not come out too badly. They are an expression of the *affectus collegialis* – that is, not the real collegial article but a warm glow of emotion not wholly unconnected with it. But the reminder that 'one should always bear in mind the inalienable responsibility of every individual bishop towards the universal Church' could be taken to mean that if Cardinal Sales wants to sing out of chorus with the episcopal conference of Brazil, then he is perfectly entitled to do so – indeed has a duty to do so. Still, further study of episcopal conferences is recommended, so it cannot be said that Ratzinger has won this round yet; on the other hand, since it looks as though this study will be conducted under his auspices, one does not need second sight to know what the answer might be.

I was able to see Cardinal Danneels on 7 December when he defended his document, claimed paternity, and challenged me to illustrate the difference between his first and his final *relatio*. On this question, the reader can make up his or her own mind on the basis of this book.

But Danneels did make one point of great importance. He claimed that the Oriental churches and the churches suffering under communism (such as Vietnam and Kampuchea) had taught everyone the vital importance of a theology of the cross. So they are now brought in to 'correct' (not repudiate) the perhaps excessive optimism of *Gaudium et Spes* twenty years before. Here is the key passage:

> The Church as communion is the sacrament of the world's salvation. . . . In this context we affirm the importance and the great relevance of the pastoral constitution *Gaudium et Spes*. At the same time we observe that the signs of our times differ to some extent from those which the Council discerned, for today anguish and suffering have increased. *All over the world today there is hunger, oppression, injustice, war, torture, terrorism and other forms of violence of every kind.* This obliges us to a new and more profound theological reflection, which interprets such signs in the light of the Gospel.
>
> *Theology of the cross.* It seems to us that in these modern difficulties God is teaching us the value, importance and centrality of the cross of Jesus Christ. Thus the relation between human history and salvation-history makes sense only in the light of the paschal mystery. *The theology of the cross, far from excluding the theology of creation and the incarnation, presupposes it.* When Christians talk about the cross, they do not deserve to be called pessimists, for we are grounded in the realism of Christian hope.

The two sentences I have italicized were late additions. One is forced to admit that if 'famine, injustice, war and torture' are to be seen as the new 'signs of the times', then the meaning of the expression has been totally changed. In Pope John's usage, followed by *Gaudium et Spes*, the signs are all positive – the growing interdependence of the world was leading to a new international order, women, workers and colonies were emancipating themselves *and* in all this the Holy Spirit was at work. The sign of the times was a coded message from the Holy Spirit. But clearly famine and terrorism cannot be read in this way. Twenty years later, there has been a return to the 'Polish proposal' (see p. 17 above) achieved in the name of 'realism' and with the support of the persecuted churches and the Oriental churches. The second italicized phrase represents a small, though important, restatement of *Gaudium et*

Spes. For any theology which wants to bring out the value of human work has to be based on the doctrine of 'creation and the incarnation'. This is acknowledged, at the last gasp, so *Gaudium et Spes* is saved.

The cat was let out of the bag when Pope John Paul right at the end of the Synod 'welcomed' the proposal that a catechism valid for the whole Church should be prepared. This he said was 'a real necessity'. But if so, then he had wanted it all along. Yet none of the preliminary reports from episcopal conferences had expressed any such desire, and we know that the Italians and French were happy with their own catechisms and had been in trouble with the Congregation of the Clergy on this very question. The request for a standard catechism came ostensibly 'from the floor' of the Synod, but it is impossible to think of it as something that welled up spontaneously, leading Ratzinger and the Pope to say, 'Goodness gracious, what an excellent idea'. Personally, I doubt whether the catechism can be completed before the year 2,000. But the symbolic issue of the universal catechism illustrates the way in which the Extraordinary Synod was used to reinforce the institutional control of the Roman Curia.

It is time to conclude. If the final report is disappointing, this is not because anything it says is false so much as because it emphasizes the wrong things. It is also loose and imprecise in its handling of language, confusing 'secularization' with 'secularism', for instance, and pronouncing the latter to be the principal 'sign of the times' of our era. It was (wrongly) said that Kasper stomped away from the Synod complaining that there had been no role for theologians. He would have certainly answered Ratzinger's and the report's point that the reason why the young regard the Church as an institution is because 'we have talked too much about Church structures and not enough about Christ and God'. But this is just plain wrong. People regard the Church as an institution because that is how they experience it. The remedy is not to talk more about Jesus but to make the local communities more welcoming, more human, more an expression of *koinonia*. The final report states the problems badly, and puts them in the wrong order.

Of course no one inside the Synod was prepared to admit this. Those who had most reason to feel they had been taken for a ride stood before television cameras and declared 'the Synod was a great success'. Bishop James W. Malone already did so on the afternoon of 6 December. There is a simple reason for this. Bishops who feel aggrieved by this Synod still have to live with it, they are not as free as I am to reveal its mechanisms, and what is more they *can* live with it. After all, they do not have to read it with the same emphasis as Ratzinger. And wise bishops – in my view the majority – know perfectly well that they cannot admit defeat when there has never, officially at least, been a contest. They know something else: while one may be allowed to make fine speeches about collegiality and the Church as mystery, the gritty reality of Church life depends upon who has control of the institutions – the nomination of bishops, the licence to teach theology, the proposal of models of holiness. The Synod of bishops has been caught up in this process of institutional control which is concerned with *who may speak*, who is allowed to have a voice. Quite simply, this Synod lost its voice – as one ought to have known it would from the moment that there was a clamp-down on the publication of the reports from episcopal conferences.

Pope John Paul was satisfied. During his homily in St Peter's on 8 December, feast of the Immaculate Conception, he said: 'The Synod has accomplished the purposes for which it was convoked: to celebrate, verify and promote the Council'. This triplet also occurs in the final document. It is very confusing. There is no problem with 'celebrate', not much with 'promote' (except that it is used in a Latin sense). But in what sense could a Synod set out to 'verify' a Council? To test its validity? Though the Latin word used is indeed *'verificare'*, its meaning seems to be rather that of 'conform' or 're-affirm'. I am grateful to Cardinal O Fiaich for pointing this out. But there remains something faintly condescending in the final document: 'Unanimously and joyfully we also verify that the Council is a legitimate and joyful expression and interpretation of the deposit of faith as it is found in sacred scripture and in the living tradition of the Church'. That is fine. But who, apart from dissident Archbishop Marcel Lefebvre and the editors of *The Wanderer*, ever thought anything else? The Synod was an expensive way of saying that the 'reception' of Vatican II had to continue. Danneels had found an image for it: 'It was like a slight adjustment on a rocket, a touch on the controls, not going into reverse'.

So there is no reason to give up hope. For the bishops will return to their churches, wiser men, and they will soon get their voices back. Cardinal Basil Hume, racing for the line at the end of chapter 6, discovered that it was a different ball game after all. But he and his friends now have a splendid opportunity to begin to realize the Church as *koinonia*. This Synod made one important decision. It

decided not to have an election for the Synod Council but to retain
the fifteen who were already preparing the ordinary Synod of 1987
before the Extraordinary Synod came along to throw them out of
joint. Was this a belated recognition of the injustice done by
excluding men such as Cardinals Bernadin, Arns and Martini? It
is possible. But they will be back and can join Cardinals Basil Hume
and Roger Etchegaray in preparing 'The Vocation and Mission of
the Laity in the Church and in the World'. Hardly anyone noticed
the most important statement made by Cardinal Eduardo Pironio,
now President of the Council for the Laity, soon to be a Congregation (or not, as the case may be). He said:

> This Synod should be a sort of solemn inauguration of the prep-
> arations for the next ordinary Synod on the laity in autumn 1987.
> The real theme of the next Synod is the Church: for it is in the
> Church that the vocation and mission of lay people are lived out.
> Moreover, the preparation for the next Synod should involve the
> whole ecclesial community, under the presidency of the bishops.

So the whole Church is to be involved from now on in this exercise.
It will be impossible to talk about the laity without consulting them,
and difficult to fix in advance a properly prepared Synod. Bishop
Bernard Hubert's vision could yet be realized: the Synod will be
extended to the whole Church through the next two years. A little
unhappiness now is a small price to pay for that.

Index

143